What's Ahead for
MALAYSIA?

What's Ahead for
MALAYSIA?
Contemporary Challenges and Emerging Trends

PHUA KAI LIT • SOO KENG SOON

Pelanduk
Publications
pelanduk.com

Published by
Pelanduk Publications (M) Sdn. Bhd.
(Co. No. 113307-W)
12 Jalan SS13/3E,
Subang Jaya Industrial Estate
47500 Subang Jaya
Selangor Darul Ehsan, Malaysia

Address all correspondence to
Pelanduk Publications (M) Sdn. Bhd.
P.O. Box 8265, 46785 Kelana Jaya
Selangor Darul Ehsan, Malaysia

Check out our website at **www.pelanduk.com**
e-mail: **rusaone@tm.net.my**

Phua, Kai Lit
    What's ahead for Malaysia? contemporary challenges and
    emerging trends / Phua Kai Lit, Soo Keng Soon.
    Includes index
    ISBN 967-978-901-2
    1. Globalization. 2. Malaysia—Economic conditions. 3. Malaysia—
    Social conditions. 4. Social change—Malaysia. 5. Malaysia—Politics
    and government. I. Soo, Keng Soon. II. Title.
    303.482595

Printed and bound in Malaysia

Contents

PART II

Preface

WE decided to write this book for a number of reasons. One reason is to make the fruits of social-science research more readily available to members of the Malaysian public. Another is to discuss major challenges that Malaysia (and Malaysians) are facing and to propose possible responses and solutions to these challenges. Thus, in Part I [written by Phua Kai Lit], various aspects of Malaysian society are discussed. In Part II [largely written by Soo Keng Soon], the concept of a "knowledge economy" and the challenges of "globalisation" are discussed, besides delving into the skills needed for professional success in a globalised economy in the 21st century. We have enjoyed writing this book and hope you will enjoy reading it too.

Phua Kai Lit, Shah Alam, Selangor
Soo Keng Soon, Dallas, Texas

PART I

Chapter 1

Population and Health

THE number of people living in Malaysia in 2004 is about 23 million. This number includes at least a million foreigners (those with legal immigration status as well as those who are in the country illegally). Although the size of the population has increased over time, the rate of population growth has slowed down in Malaysia as the people begin to marry at older ages, have children later in their marriages and also have fewer children per family. People marry later and postpone having children because they spend more years in school nowadays and also because they wish to spend more time on building up their careers first. This is especially true of women who are highly educated. The general trend is that the more highly educated a woman is, the later she will marry and the fewer children she will be likely to have.

A few generations ago, it was common for women to get married in their teens and to start bearing children very soon after marriage. Few women were given the chance to acquire higher education. Today, Malaysian women are more likely to study beyond secondary school and to work outside the home upon completion of their studies. Hence, women tend to marry later and to start having babies later.

Women have fewer children nowadays (especially Malaysians of Chinese ancestry) because of changing social norms and values as well as pragmatic reasons such as the difficulties of balancing a career outside the home with the domestic duties of being a good wife and being a good mother to the children. ("Norms" is a term used by social scientists to refer to what is considered "appropriate behaviour" or "socially approved behaviour" in a particular community or society while "values" refer to what is considered to be morally "good" or "bad".) Among the older generations of Malaysians, a large number of children, usually male children, was considered to be a blessing. This, coupled with the lack of effective methods of birth control, therefore encouraged the formation of large families in the past. However, as women gained greater access to higher education and to better job opportunities, it became less desirable to have a large number of kids. The appearance of highly effective methods of birth control such as the contraceptive pill also made it easier for a woman to plan the number of children she would like to have. Hence the appearance of families with fewer children today.

Nevertheless, whatever the size of their families, all working women have to deal with the so-called "Double

Burden of Women" and the "Supermom Syndrome". The "Double Burden of Women" refers to the fact that women who work outside the home also tend to shoulder most of the burden of domestic duties and responsibilities such as caring for the children and doing the cooking and the housework while the "Supermom Syndrome" refers to pressure on a woman to be an exemplary worker in the eyes of the boss, a loving wife and companion to her husband and a devoted and loving mother in the eyes of her children—all at the same time. In the Malaysian context, there is also pressure to be a "good daughter-in-law" (however it is defined) to her husband's parents. The "Double Burden of Women" and the "Supermom Syndrome" may thus result in a lot of time, physical and psychological pressure on today's working Malaysian woman.

As women become better and better educated and they begin to rise higher and higher in the working world, their work responsibilities would increase and their working hours would also get longer and longer. It is easier on a career woman if she has only one or two kids rather than a large number of kids. Gone are the days when Malaysian Chinese women married in their teens, became housewives and had five, six, seven or more children: the number of kids is likely to be three or fewer nowadays. Working women who have their mothers living with them (traditionally, Malaysian Malay mothers tend to stay with their married daughters and help to take care of the grandchildren) are the luckier ones since the latter can help to shoulder some of the burden of looking after the kids in the family. Working women who have a live-in mother-in-law can also benefit in similar ways. However, these women may experience even more difficulties if they do not get along with their mothers-in-law! Tensed relations with their live-in mothers-in-law would increase the level of stress in their lives. This is more likely to be the case if the live-in mother-in-law is more traditional in her thinking while the daughter-in-law thinks differently and does not agree with traditional ideas such as showing deference and being obedient to her husband's mother.

It is common nowadays for middle-class and upper-class Malaysians to hire maids from foreign countries such as Indonesia and the Philippines to do the housework and help to take care of the children. A maid relieves some of the pressure on the working mother. Nevertheless, this is not an ideal solution since the maid may be left alone with the children while the mother and father are both working at the office—the children may be neglected by the maid or even worse may occur. When both parents are at work outside the home, the children are essentially left to their own devices, unsupervised (if there are no live-in grandparents), even if there happens to be a maid in the house. There is essentially nobody to discipline the kids and to make sure that they stay out of trouble if they are teenagers. Some social science experts who study the family are troubled by this fact and believe that it can contribute to feelings of neglect and alienation on the part of children. Some may even grow up to be troubled teenagers.

Another reason why people are having fewer children is because as people migrate from the countryside and the small towns to live and work in the big towns and cities of

Malaysia, it becomes more and more expensive to bring up their children. In the countryside, children are economically productive at relatively young ages. They can help with padi farming, weeding, looking after younger brothers and sisters, helping out with domestic duties, looking after the cows, buffaloes, goats, ducks and chickens and so on and contribute to the financial well-being of the family in other ways. But in the cities, children are less likely to be able to contribute economically to the family. They spend a lot of time in school and on school-related activities. Besides this, they are unlikely to be working unless their parents are running a family business and need assistance from the children. Therefore, it makes sense for city people to have fewer children while "investing" more in each of them. Thus, middle-class Malaysian parents nowadays typically push their children to do well in school and they also spend sizeable amounts of money on their children for extra tuition classes, music lessons and so on.

Malaysian society has changed a lot over the past few decades. Nowadays, cohabitation (unmarried couples living together and having a sexual relationship) is found in big cities such as Kuala Lumpur and its surrounding suburbs. This was practically unheard of in the 1960s and 1970s. For good or ill, this behaviour is a cultural adaptation from certain Western countries where cohabitation is relatively common. Divorce rates are rising in Malaysia. Malays have traditionally had relatively high divorce rates while divorce was very rare among the Chinese and the Indians because of strong social pressures against it. However, with rising educational levels among non-Malay women and their growing financial independence because of paid work outside the home, they are finding the option of dissolving unsatisfactory or abusive marriages more viable. Hence the rising divorce rates among non-Malays. However, divorcees continue to be stigmatised in Malaysia and divorced women are especially disadvantaged; it is difficult for them to get married again for various reasons. Divorced women who are middle aged and who have kids are truly handicapped in terms of finding another partner and remarrying in the "marriage market". This is because the vast majority of men around their age would already have been married. Malaysian social prejudices also prevent them from marrying men who are significantly younger (this, however, does not apply to divorced men since men can marry much younger women). Unless they are willing to marry a man who is a widower or a divorcee, they will have much difficulty in finding a second husband. Female divorcees are further disadvantaged if they stopped their schooling when they got married and if they had also decided to stop working to raise their kids for a few years before going back into the labour force. If they get divorced, they would have low educational qualifications and inadequate work experience. This would make them less attractive to potential employers.

One development in neighbouring Singapore (which is probably also beginning to occur in Malaysia) is the phenomenon of highly educated women having problems finding "suitable" husbands and lowly educated men having problems finding wives. Therefore, unless there are changes in social attitudes such as "a woman should marry 'up' in terms of marrying a man who is better educated and who earns more money" and "a man should marry 'down' in terms of marrying a woman who is less well educated and earns less money", there will be more and more singles to be found among the ranks of highly educated women and lowly educated men in Malaysia.

Ageing population

As mentioned earlier, Malaysian couples are having fewer children on the average. This results in a falling birth rate which, in turn, gives rise to the problem of ageing of the population, i.e., because fewer children are being born, the percentage of old people in the Malaysian population rises steadily over time. According to the national Population and Housing Census carried out in 2000, Malaysians over age 65 make up 3.9 per cent of the total population of 23.27 million. Another way of approaching this subject is to look at the absolute number of senior citizens in Malaysia. A simple calculation shows that there were already more than 900,000 Malaysians over age 65 in 2000 (i.e., 3.9 per cent of a total population of 23.27 million).

Population experts at the United Nations have projected that this will increase to 9 per cent in 2025 and 15.4 per cent in 2050. The percentage is likely to rise to over 20 per cent beyond 2050, i.e., one in every five Malaysians in the future will be an elderly person. What is likely to happen as the Malaysian population ages? As the population ages, we can expect the demand for services used heavily by the elderly to increase. These would include dental and health services (including demand for pharmaceutical products), leisure services such as tourism, nursing homes and related social-welfare services and so on. Thus, these sectors of the economy are likely to boom in the near future. Because of ageing population, Malaysia would also need larger numbers of doctors and nurses who specialise in treating the elderly, nursing home aides, home health workers and so on. There would also be greater pressure on the social services system of Malaysia since most of the elderly would be retirees who are not working and need to be supported by working Malaysians through the taxes paid by the latter.

Urbanisation and migration

Malaysia is also getting more urbanised, i.e., more and more people are moving from the countryside to live and work in the bigger towns and cities. Indeed, it is likely that much of the residents of major Malaysian towns and cities such as Kuala Lumpur, Penang, Johor Baru, Kuching and Kota Kinabalu were born elsewhere and moved to these big towns because of better educational and work opportunities. Thus, industrial development in the Klang Valley, various areas of Penang Island and around Johor Baru has been accompanied by migration and rapid population increase. Hence, we witness the phenomenon of "emptying out" of the cities during major festivals such as Hari Raya Aidil Fitri and the Chinese New Year. Suddenly, there are no more of the infamous and much dreaded traffic jams in the big cities. Many of the residents of the major towns and cities are on their way home to celebrate the festivities with their relatives in smaller towns elsewhere or in the rural areas. Thus, during a festival such as Hari Raya Aidil Fitri, smaller towns such as Kota Baru begin to experience traffic jams as native sons and daughters return from out of town for a few days!

We mentioned in-migration and population increase earlier. In the case of Johor Baru, the availability of higher-paying jobs in nearby Singapore has also been an important factor in its population increase. Malaysians who live in Johor Baru can commute daily to work in Singapore. Indeed, during each weekday morning, the number of Malaysians travelling into Singapore to work is considerable and can number in the tens of thousands. This causes massive traffic congestion and significant air and noise pollution at the Causeway.

The shift in population from the countryside and small towns to the more economically dynamic big towns and cities such as Kuala Lumpur, Penang and Johor Baru has, however, given rise to problems such as overcrowding, traffic jams, inflation in the price of essential goods such as housing, greater strain on services such as electricity, water supply, sanitation and garbage collection and so on. It has also contributed to the problem of "urban sprawl", i.e., the cities keep expanding outward and the suburbs keep growing and growing. It becomes more and more difficult to identify where one city ends and where the next begins. This is especially evident when one drives from Kuala Lumpur to Port Klang via Petaling Jaya, Subang Jaya, Shah Alam and Klang. Each day, more and more of the surrounding countryside and roadside palm oil and rubber plantations disappear to be replaced by roads, housing estates, factories, shops and so on. There seems to be no end to the "concrete jungle" as greenery (whether in the form of jungle, rubber plantations or oil palm plantations) .

disappears to be replaced by more and more areas of concrete. Some Malaysians may consider this to be "development" while those who consider themselves to be environmentalists would be dismayed by such developments.

People who migrate to the cities but who are poorly educated or unskilled are likely to end up with low-paying jobs and live in poor quality or squatter housing. Migrants who are highly educated or highly skilled tend to secure better-paying jobs but are likely to end up in a housing market where the price of housing seems to go up year after year. Indeed, house prices in the Klang Valley and in Johor Baru are among the highest in Malaysia. Thus, some of the gains derived from holding higher-paying city jobs are cancelled by the higher prices in the major towns and cities. Besides this, it is also likely that migrants would find living and working in the city to be more psychologically stressful than life in the countryside and small towns. Thus, after their retirement, these migrants are likely to return to their *kampungs* and small towns in Kelantan, Terengganu, Pahang, Kedah and so on. Meanwhile, the *kampungs* and small towns continue to experience outflows of their young people and also an ageing of the remaining population.

As mentioned earlier, Malaysians are moving from the countryside to the towns and cities. However, some are going beyond these—they are migrating overseas to Singapore, Australia, New Zealand, Britain and North America. There have also been reports of Malaysians migrating to work illegally in Taiwan and Japan. Some overseas Malaysians are students who decided to stay behind after completion of their higher education in countries like Australia and the U.S. Others are those who decided to work overseas because of the higher pay or because overseas earnings seem higher when converted into Malaysian ringgit. Whatever their reasons may be, if the number of highly-educated and highly-skilled Malaysians working overseas is high, this would result in a significant "brain drain" problem for the country, i.e., some of our best brains would have drained out and their potential contributions to Malaysian society and to the Malaysian economy are lost. However, the bright side of the picture is that overseas Malaysians do contribute to the Malaysian economy indirectly by remitting money home. Others contribute by serving as economic and cultural "bridges" between Malaysia and the foreign country where they have settled down. Thus, a Malaysian living in Australia may establish his or her own business and contribute to greater trade between Malaysia and Australia through the operations of the new business. Other "Overseas Malaysians" can also contribute when and if they finally return home to work after acquiring new skills and mastering the latest technology while working overseas.

The polar opposite of emigration of Malaysians to foreign countries is, of course, immigration of foreigners into Malaysia. Foreign workers in Malaysia can be classified by skill level and by legal status. They can be skilled or unskilled and legal or illegal. These two categories can also overlap, i.e., there can be "skilled, legal" foreign workers as well as "skilled, illegal" foreign workers (such as those who enter Malaysia on a social visit pass but who engage in consultancy or professional work while in the country). There can also be "unskilled, legal" and "unskilled, illegal" workers. The controversy over immigrant workers deals more with those who are unskilled (especially those who are unskilled as well as of illegal status). The Malaysian Trades Union Congress (MTUC) opposes continued entry of unskilled foreign workers into the country because of the downward pressure exerted on wage levels by large numbers of foreigners who are willing to work for lower wages than Malaysian citizens. Employers, on the other hand, support the continued influx of foreign workers since they can lower their labour costs by employing these lower-priced foreigners. Another argument from the employers is that without foreigners, "undesirable" jobs would go unfilled since Malaysians allegedly shun them and that even the survival of some industries would be threatened, e.g., labour-intensive sectors such as oil palm plantations. It should also not be forgotten that unskilled immigrant labour includes maids and other domestic workers from Indonesia and the Philippines. Their presence in Malaysia allows local women to work outside the home in full-time jobs. Rightly or wrongly, the continued influx of unskilled, illegal foreign workers (such as those from Sumatra and Java into Peninsular Malaysia and those from Kalimantan and Mindanao into East Malaysia) is perceived as a major problem by many Malaysians.

Health of the population

All these forms of population changes (falling birth rates and ageing population, urbanisation of the Malaysian population, and immigration of foreign workers) are related to changes in Malaysian health indicators. Two commonly used indicators of the health status of a population are the "infant mortality rate" and the "life expectancy rate". The infant mortality rate gives an idea of how many babies die before they reach their first birthday. The life expectancy rate gives us an idea of how long men and women are likely to live, on the average. As the standard of living in Malaysia rises (higher income and education levels, better housing with piped water and proper sanitation facilities, better access to basic healthcare services), these health indicators have steadily improved. The Malaysian infant mortality rate is less than 8 per thousand live births and continues to fall from year to year while the life expectancy rates for both men and women continue to increase. However, although the "diseases of poverty" (such as diseases due to malnutrition like beri-beri and diseases due to contaminated water supply and poor sanitation like cholera) are declining in importance, diseases associated with affluence and population ageing are increasing in importance. As income levels rise, the diet of some segments of the Malaysian population becomes more and more like the "Western" pattern with high levels of protein, fat, sugar and salt intake and this results in higher rates of obesity, heart and circulatory diseases, stroke, diabetes and so on. Other major killers of Malaysians include cancer, injuries such as road-traffic accidents and suicides. Cancer is related to higher rates of smoking (e.g., lung cancer), ageing population, industrialisation and very likely, to changes in diet and to higher levels of environmental pollution. Certain forms of cancer are linked to increased occupational exposure to dangerous chemicals as a result of the growing number of industrial and construction jobs in Malaysia. The larger number of deaths and disabilities due to road-traffic accidents is due to the larger number of vehicles on the road, the larger number of young drivers and to higher driving speeds on the roads. Motorcycle riders are at higher risk of being killed or maimed in road-traffic accidents than motorists. Young, male motorists and young, male motorcycle riders are at especially high risk because of lack of driving experience and their greater propensity for risk-taking behaviour on the roads and highways of Malaysia. The drinking of alcohol further increases the risk of road-traffic injuries. We should be concerned because Malaysia has one of the highest rates of road-traffic injuries in the world. Such injuries and deaths generate significant economic and social costs both to the affected individuals and their families, as well as to the nation.

Suicides have gained in importance as a leading cause of death because of the decline in infectious diseases and because many of the diseases which affect the ageing population are chronic diseases which do not result in quick death. Thus, although rates of heart disease, stroke, diabetes, etc. are rising, people who suffer from these can continue to live for many years although their "quality of life" is adversely affected. Quality of life refers to the following: physical well-being, emotional well-being, social well-being, and the ability to carry out "Activities of Daily Living" (ADL) such as getting out of bed, going to the toilet, grooming oneself, eating, walking, bathing and so on.

There is also growing recognition of the problem of domestic violence or violence within families. The term "domestic violence" is usually used to refer to cases of one spouse beating up another. However, it can also include cases of physical abuse of children by their parents, physical abuse of the elderly by younger family members and physical abuse of maids by their employers. Domestic violence victims (who tend to be female) can suffer severe injuries or even death at the hands of family members. There can also be other forms of abuse within troubled families, i.e., neglect of kids, verbal abuse, psychological abuse and even sexual abuse of kids by other family members. Domestic violence is a social problem which needs to be tackled seriously because it can lead to lasting negative effects in its victims (especially in those who were abused as children). These negative effects include behavioural problems in children and personality disorders in adults.

As the pattern of diseases changes from infectious diseases to chronic diseases, Malaysia needs to deal with the emerging problem of how to organise, finance and provide healthcare and social services to greater numbers of young invalids (due mainly to road accidents and job-related injuries) and elderly people with long-term illnesses. There is a trend of rising healthcare costs and unless the government takes effective action to control healthcare cost inflation or continue to provide heavily subsidised health services to the people, this would be a problem that all Malaysians will have to face in the near future.

Malaysia also has a significant problem of drug abuse and drug addiction in relation to our population. Although drug addicts are disproportionately Malay, in recent years, there have been reports of growing abuse of a drug called "Ecstasy" (methamphetamine) by Chinese teenagers and youths. This is worrisome because Ecstasy abuse can lead to permanent brain damage. The drug abuse problem is also linked to the problem of rising cases of HIV/AIDS in the country. The virus which attacks the immune system of the human body and gives rise to AIDS can be spread through the exchange of contaminated needles used to inject drugs. Thus, drug addicts who share needles are at high risk of contracting the HIV virus. The virus can also be transmitted through sexual contact. Hence, drug addicts who engage in prostitution to earn money to pay for drugs are at higher risk of contracting the virus or can easily spread the virus if they themselves are already HIV positive. Crime rates can also increase if drug abusers resort to petty theft and to robberies in order to get money to feed their addictions. It should also be pointed out that people who are HIV positive are at greater risk of being affected by tuberculosis. Thus, as the number of HIV cases rise, the number of TB cases will also rise.

From the public health point of view, immigrant workers from poor countries can also "import" infectious diseases such as tuberculosis into Malaysia. Thus, foreign workers should be carefully screened for infectious diseases before being allowed into the country. A new development in the region (beginning in the early 1990s) is the phenomenon of cross-border air pollution, i.e., the notorious "haze" originating in Indonesia (Sumatra and Kalimantan) and blowing into Malaysia, Singapore, southern Thailand and Brunei. Although Indonesian peasants who practice slash-and-burn or swidden agriculture are often accused of being the cause of the problem, there have been reports that multinational agricultural companies (e.g., Malaysian companies operating in Indonesia) are actually the main culprits. Apparently these companies resort to burning of cleared vegetation prior to planting of oil palm because it is cheaper to do so. The haze is an important health hazard for children, the elderly and those who suffer from chronic respiratory and cardiovascular diseases as prolonged exposure to it is the equivalent of smoking many packs of cigarettes in a day.

In Malaysia today, the health status of certain subgroups tend to be significantly poorer than the health status of the majority, e.g., the *Orang Asli*, estate workers, urban squatters and immigrants (especially illegal immigrants). Much can be done to improve the health of these subgroups.

Chapter 2

Education

MALAYSIA has managed to achieve high rates of literacy among its younger generations. This is something to be proud of indeed since many Third World countries, including neighbouring countries such as Indonesia, continue to be affected by high rates of illiteracy (especially among the female population). Economists who specialise in "development economics" (a branch of economics devoted to the study of the problems of economic development of poor countries) believe that investment in the education of females gives rise to significant societal benefits. The education of females is strongly associated with declining infant mortality rates and under-5 mortality rates (deaths of babies under age 1 and deaths of babies under age 5 respectively). In other words, educated women—even those with only a primary or lower secondary education—make better mothers. Educated mothers are more aware of proper nutrition for their children and of the importance of good hygiene in childcare. Educated females can also contribute to economic growth by participating in the labour force. Thus, many of Malaysia's industrial workers are young females. This is especially true in export-oriented industries such as the electronics industry. These young female workers are the unsung heroines in Malaysia's rapid industrialisation over the course of the last few decades. A simple way to confirm the major role played by young women in Malaysia's industrialisation over the last few decades is to station oneself near the gates of electronics factories in Petaling Jaya or Bayan Lepas and to note the large numbers of young women pouring out of the gates at the end of work shifts.

Malaysia's younger generations are spending more and more years in school. This is necessary as the structure of the economy changes as Malaysia industrialises and moves from primary industries (agriculture, fishing, mining and forestry) to secondary industries such as manufacturing of cars, electrical and computer equipment and tertiary services like tourism, banking, insurance and other financial services. Secondary and tertiary industries require higher levels of education and literacy (including computer literacy) than the primary industries. Industrial development also requires higher numbers of better educated workers. These not only include scientists, engineers and managers but also middle-level executives and skilled and semi-skilled blue-collar workers.

Thus, in the last few decades, the Malaysian government has not only expanded the number of tertiary/post-secondary institutions of education such as polytechnics and public universities (including branch campuses) from the original few such as Universiti Malaya, Universiti Sains Malaysia, Universiti Kebangsaan Malaysia, Universiti Pertanian Malaysia (now Universiti Putra Malaysia) and Universiti Teknologi Malaysia but it has also encouraged the growth of the private sector in higher education. New public sector universities such as Universiti Utara Malaysia, Universiti Malaysia Sarawak and Universiti Malaysia Sabah have been established while colleges like Institut Teknologi Mara have been upgraded to university status. The private sector has been permitted to establish numerous tertiary level colleges offering diploma and degree courses. One of the first diploma-granting private colleges to be established was the Tunku Abdul Rahman College. Subsequently, private-sector colleges were allowed to establish twinning programmes with foreign universities whereby Malaysian students completed the first part of their course in the Malaysian private college and then travelled to the foreign university to complete the rest of the academic course. Their degrees would be awarded by the foreign university partner in the twinning programme. In more recent years, Malaysian private colleges began offering "3+0" programmes where students can study for their franchised foreign university degrees entirely in Malaysia. Private-sector colleges are also offering franchised degree courses from local universities such as Universiti Sains Malaysia. Universities established by private-sector corporations include those set up by Telekom Malaysia (Multimedia University in Cyberjaya), Tenaga Nasional Malaysia and Petronas. Universiti Tunku Abdul Rahman (UTAR) is another private university which was established recently. The International Medical University is a private-sector institution that offers twinning medical and pharmacy programmes with foreign universities. It also offers its own undergraduate medical degree. An "open university" has also been established (Universiti Terbuka) based on the British model.

Malaysian students have traditionally sought higher education in relatively large numbers in Britain, Canada, Australia, New Zealand, the Middle East and also in neighbouring countries like Singapore, India and Indonesia. The large numbers of Malaysian students studying overseas is a strong indicator of "demand" for university places exceeding the "supply". It is also a major contributor to currency outflow from the country. Thus, the government has encouraged the establishment of twinning programmes, 3+0 programmes and private, degree-granting universities to reduce this outflow. Foreign universities such as Monash University from Australia have even been permitted to open branch campuses in Malaysia.

Local institutions of tertiary education are attracting more and more foreign students to study in Malaysia. This is a positive development in that it contributes to the Malaysian economy and also promotes interaction between local students and foreign students. Cross-cultural interaction will help to make our students more sophisticated as well as promote the building of interpersonal networks that will be useful in the future when they engage in international diplomatic, economic or sociocultural activities. We may also be able to attract "foreign talent" by getting smart foreign students to study in Malaysia, i.e., if they decide to work in Malaysia for a few years or even permanently after graduation. The inflow of foreign-born talent is one important factor in the prowess of American scientific and technological research. There is no reason why Malaysia cannot emulate the Americans in this respect.

The importance of adult and continuing education

There is a boom in adult and continuing education. For example, people who are already in the work force may enroll in part-time courses to earn degrees in information technology or business management. This is a good thing since lifelong learning is becoming more and more important with rapid changes in technology and changes in the structure of the job market because of "globalisation". Rapid changes in technology can give rise to "technological obsolescence" and result in the disappearance of jobs. Hence the importance of lifelong learning and the constant upgrading of job-related skills.

More use of English

One major aspect of globalisation is the increasing integration of the economies of the world through trade, foreign investment, labour flows and so on. Another aspect is the importance of languages such as English in international business. Thus, the government has permitted greater usage of English in Malaysian education. For example, English is often the medium of instruction in private-sector tertiary-level colleges and universities. The government recognises that English has become a major language in international business and mastery of English is essential in order for Malaysians to keep up with the latest scientific and technological advances. Language policy has always been a difficult and controversial issue in Malaysian politics. Thus, the increased use of English in education in Malaysia shows that the government is actually quite pragmatic and willing to adapt to changed circumstances although this change in policy has caused unhappiness among certain groups of cultural nationalists. The cultural nationalists include those who believe that more emphasis on English will erode the status of Malay as the national language. There are also those who oppose the use of English in teaching science and mathematics in the Chinese-language public schools for their own particular reasons. In our opinion, such opposition is unwise because the increased use of English will not displace Malay as the national language. Neither will it displace Mandarin Chinese in the Chinese-language public schools. Instead, fluency in English will enable Malaysians to obtain jobs more easily (whether in the local job market or in foreign job markets), facilitate business dealings with foreigners and also help us to keep up with technical advances more easily. Today, even the Japanese government is pushing its citizens to improve their fluency in English in order to better reap the benefits of globalisation. Blind cultural and linguistic nationalism would only damage the welfare of Malaysians in the long run. (In fact, it is already being reported that graduates of Malaysian public universities who are weak in English are experiencing difficulty in getting jobs in the private sector in Malaysia.)

Continuing inadequacies

Malaysia has come a long way from the situation which existed before the racial riots of May 13, 1969 during which Malays were overrepresented among the ranks of the poor and the number of Malays in professional and managerial occupations was very low. Whatever the pros and cons of the controversial, pro-*Bumiputera* affirmative action programmes of the New Economic Policy (NEP), the fact is that a Malay middle class has emerged and it is no longer uncommon to find Malay professionals and high-level managers with tertiary-level educational qualifications. This has undoubtedly reduced the level of ethnic tension and contributed to greater social harmony in the country. However, other ethnic groups such as the *Orang Asli* and East Malaysian natives continue to remain significantly disadvantaged compared to the Malays and the Chinese in terms of educational and occupational achievement. It appears that the Indians in Malaysia are also becoming another educationally disadvantaged group—this is especially true of those who attend Tamil-language primary schools in the rural areas. Perhaps it is time the government takes more drastic action in order to improve their lot in Malaysian society.

In spite of all these gains, certain problems remain in the Malaysian school system. There continues to be an overemphasis on the learning of facts in order to pass examinations (especially national examinations at the end of Forms Three, Five and Six). There is also the "rote learning" problem which results in secondary school and even university graduates who are weak in critical thinking skills and who are not very effective at doing research and solving problems independently. The Singaporean government has recognised this problem and is revamping its educational system to reduce rote learning and to promote critical thinking and research skills. Education policymakers in Malaysia should keep an eye on this revamping of the Singaporean educational system and see what can be done in order to emulate their successes and avoid their failures.

Another problem is ethnic segregation in the Malaysian school system. This is especially true in the private "Islamic" kindergartens and schools, public Islamic schools (*Sekolah Kebangsaan Agama*), public "National Type" Mandarin Chinese-language, and public "National Type" Tamil-language primary schools. It is also true in the parallel, independent (non-government) Chinese secondary school system in Malaysia. The Islamic schools, whether private or public, are overwhelmingly Malay in composition. Similarly, the National Type Chinese-language schools consist mostly of Chinese students while the National Type Tamil-language schools consist mostly of Indian students. However, a positive development is the increasing number of non-Chinese students who have been enrolled by their parents to study in the Chinese-language schools. The continued existence of Chinese-language and Tamil-language schools is positive from the point of view of multiculturalism but it does make the goal of eventually developing a Malaysian population that is fluent both in the national language (Malay) and in the international language English more difficult to achieve. The Islamic schools help to promote religious segregation and unfortunately, may even promote intolerance towards other religious faiths in Malaysia.

Problem of credentialism ("diploma disease")

There is also the problem of credentialism in Malaysia. Credentialism, also called the "diploma disease" by a British scholar named Ronald Dore, refers to the interest of students in accumulating tertiary-level educational credentials for the sake of accumulation alone. A tertiary-level educational credential is seen purely as a means of securing a higher paying job. There is no real interest in learning for the sake of acquiring knowledge or for broadening the mind. All sorts of shortcuts and strategies are used to pass exams and to get an educational credential as quickly and as cheaply as possible. Thus, although a person may possess a tertiary-level diploma or degree, he or she may not actually possess all the skills and knowledge which the diploma or degree is supposed to certify. It is very likely that as the number of people with an undergraduate degree increases in Malaysia, the "educational arms race" will intensify and people will attempt to possess at least Masters level credentials in order to differentiate themselves from the rest of the pack in the job market. The current, examination-oriented system of primary and secondary education in Malaysia stifles the interest of students in learning for the sake of learning and is a major contributing factor to the "Diploma Disease".

One question which the educational authorities need to ponder is whether our education system is producing the "appropriate" mix of secondary school and tertiary-level graduates necessary for the new technology and knowledge-based economy. Some believe that Malaysian universities are producing too many arts graduates and that the number of science and technology graduates should be increased. Others believe that this is not a major problem since properly-trained arts graduates are flexible and adaptable and can succeed in the world of commerce as managers and entrepreneurs. Thus, arts graduates who practise self-education and lifelong learning can contribute as much to the Malaysian economy as science and technology graduates in the long run. Indeed, lifelong learning and flexibility are necessary for employees to stay competitive in future job markets. Science and technology graduates who do not keep up with the latest scientific and technological advances will find that their skills have become obsolete and will experience difficulty in retaining or changing their jobs. Some social science researchers in the U.S. believe that the days of lifelong employment with a single employer are over and that the average American can expect to change jobs as much as five times in his or her working life. If this view is correct, Malaysian workers should expect multiple job changes during their working lives and will therefore need to practise lifelong and independent learning. The government can facilitate this by encouraging adult and continuing education in Malaysia. The Malaysian higher education system also needs to make adult and continuing education smoother by introducing a "credit transfer" system. For example, if a person takes a computer science course for academic credit in one educational institution at a certain time and successfully completes the course, he or she should be able to transfer the credits earned to another school's computer science degree programme later on.

Higher education and research and development (R&D) in Malaysia

The higher education sector can also contribute to Malaysia's economic development through scientific and technological research and development (R&D). Research institutes in the universities, as well as those located outside such as the Rubber Research Institute of Malaysia (RRIM), can contribute by producing new technology which can be commercialised or utilised in industrial production. Biotechnology and microelectronics are two promising growth sectors of the 21st century that should be actively encouraged in Malaysia. The Cuban government has built up a thriving biotechnology industry from scratch and the Indian government has also built up a major microelectronics (software engineering) centre around the city of Bangalore in South India. Malaysia's plans for a "Multimedia Super Corridor" of high-tech, micro-electronics industries are commendable. However, in the long run, this plan is much more viable if an indigenous sector is actively and strongly encouraged to develop and if the success of the MSC does not have to depend so much on foreign investors. Furthermore, other nations have launched similar projects and the competition for foreign investors and for foreign brains is fierce indeed. The Malaysian government can also learn from the Cubans and try to build up a biotechnology sector in its Biovalley project. The educational system of Malaysia can be revamped and harnessed to promote the growth of these two sectors by encouraging entrepreneurship, increasing the number of graduates with the necessary skills and by encouraging research and development in these areas. We have discussed the brain-drain problem in the chapter on "Population and Health" earlier. Therefore, another smart step would be to encourage the return of highly skilled Malaysians who are working in these high-technology industries in Singapore or in California's Silicon Valley and Massachusetts' Route 128. This would counter the negative effects of the "brain drain" problem (discussed earlier) to some extent.

Chapter 3

Government
and Politics

MALAYSIA possesses a political system which shows clearly the continued influence of its former colonial master Britain. There is the office of the Prime Minister and a Parliament with an appointed upper house called the "Dewan Negara" and an elected lower house called the "Dewan Rakyat". The court system is based on that of Britain and the laws of the country show strong signs of British influence. (There is, of course, the additional Syariah court system for Malaysian Muslims.) Unlike the American system of government with its "separation of powers" and "checks and balances" whereby power is divided, at the federal level, between the President, the Congress and the federal courts (with the Supreme Court at the top), power in the British parliamentary system of government tends to be concentrated to a significant degree in the hands of the Prime Minister (who is also the leader of the dominant political party or coalition of political parties in the Parliament) and the Cabinet of ministers. If the personality of the Prime Minister is strong, e.g., Lee Kuan Yew in Singapore, Margaret Thatcher in Britain and Dr Mahathir Mohamad in Malaysia, power becomes even more concentrated in the hands of the Prime Minister. Other things handed down from the past include controversial laws like the Sedition Act of 1948 and the Internal Security Act of 1960. The ISA was based on emergency regulations introduced to combat the Communist insurgency of 1948-1960 and which allows for detention without trial. Critics of laws such as the ISA argue that they should be abolished because such laws can be abused easily by the Minister of Home Affairs or used by the government of the day to stifle political dissent or suppress potential threats to their rule. They also argue that, instead, people who have been arrested under the ISA should be charged in court under other existing laws.

The Malaysian bureaucracy or civil service is relatively effective compared to those of many Third World countries. In the contemporary nation state, a public bureaucracy is absolutely necessary in order to keep the system going and to implement the policies of the government of the day. High-level bureaucrats and bureaucrats in influential public bodies, e.g., the Economic Planning Unit (EPU) in the Prime Minister's Department of Malaysia, may even take an active part behind the scenes in the formulation of new public policies. However, critics note that the bureaucracy does have a tendency to grow in size over time and unless constant action is taken to push civil servants to be efficient and productive, the bureaucracy may stagnate since it is not subjected to the competitive pressures of the marketplace. It is also necessary that the civil service not be hopelessly riddled with corruption in order for the system to function in a satisfactory manner.

The Malaysian armed forces (together with the Royal Malaysian Police) played a major role in fighting the Communist insurgency of 1948-1960 and in defending the country during the "Confrontation" with Indonesia. Fortunately for us, the armed forces have remained apolitical and have not shown any inclination to intervene in politics and neither have we been afflicted by military coups or attempted coups as in many Third World countries in Asia, Africa and Latin America. The experiences of many Third World countries show that it is relatively easy for soldiers to seize power from civilian governments. This is because the military operate through hierarchical, disciplined and well-organised bodies and also possesses the firepower with which it can use to maintain its power after a coup d'etat and to repel civilian opponents. However, the record also shows that military governments are usually heavy-handed and authoritarian and human-rights abuses are common under such governments. Although soldiers in Third World countries often seize power from corrupt civilian governments (or to prevent the territorial disintegration of the nation or to protect the resources or position of the armed forces as an institution in the country), they usually end up being equally corrupt and often make things worse for the entire country by wasting large amounts of money by purchasing sophisticated and expensive weapons and other armaments from foreign countries. Far too often, the armed forces in Third World countries end up repressing their own civilian population rather than defending the nation against military aggression by foreign countries. A good example is the armed forces of Myanmar. Malaysia is fortunate to have military and police forces (including the paramilitary General Operations Force once known as the Police Field Force) which are firmly under the control of civilians.

Internal politics and relations with neighbouring countries

The history of Malaya, and subsequently Malaysia, has been tumultuous. Malaya achieved independence from the British in 1957 in the midst of an insurgency led by the Malayan Communist Party (MCP). Malaysia was formed in 1963 when Singapore, British North Borneo (renamed Sabah) and Sarawak joined the federation. The formation of Malaysia was accompanied by a hostile reception from neighbouring Indonesia and the Philippines. Low-intensity conflict with Indonesia (the "Confrontation") did not end until after the coup against Indonesian President Sukarno that was launched by his armed forces in 1965. The Philippines has not renounced its claim to Sabah. Fortunately, lingering tension between Malaysia and the Philippines over the latter's claim to Sabah has not escalated into armed conflict. Singapore was expelled from the Federation of Malaysia in 1965 after two years of tensed relations between the city-state and the federal government. Malaysia-Singapore relations have been prickly ever since. In 1964, Singapore was stricken by race riots between Chinese and Malays. Unfortunately, the same thing happened in Malaysia five years later in May 1969 immediately after the general election. The "May 13" racial riots shook up the country and resulted in the formulation and implementation of the NEP and strong (and controversial) affirmative-action plans to improve the educational and economic standing of the Malays *vis-à-vis* the Chinese. It also resulted in an expansion of the ruling Alliance government from the original three ethnic-based political parties, i.e., the United Malays National Organisation (UMNO), the Malaysian Chinese Association (MCA) and the Malaysian Indian Congress (MIC) to the multi-party coalition called the Barisan Nasional (or National Front). The Barisan Nasional continues to dominate Malaysian politics to this day. Also, UMNO continues to be the dominant political party within the Barisan Nasional coalition of political parties. For a few years, the opposition Parti Islam SeMalaysia (PAS, or the Pan Malaysian Islamic Party) was also a member of the Barisan Nasional. Although there have been no further racial incidents comparable in severity to the 1969 race riots since, tension between the major ethnic groups persists and lie dormant below the seemingly placid surface of Malaysian society. Even so, Malaysia has been relatively successful in its management of ethnic tensions. Malaysia, Guyana and Fiji are classic examples of countries where relations between two major ethnic groups have to be managed and a satisfactory formula for power-sharing and reduction of interethnic educational and occupational inequalities has to be worked out. Guyana's challenge is to manage relations between its black population and its East Indian population. Similarly, Fiji has to manage relations between its native Fijian population and its East Indian population while Malaysia has to manage relations between its Malays and the Chinese (while not forgetting the situation of other ethnic groups such as Indians and indigenous groups in Peninsular Malaysia and East Malaysia). Malaysia's record after 1969 has been relatively successful but the management of race relations continues to be a major challenge for the Malaysian government and for all Malaysians of goodwill.

Islamic revivalism

There has been an Islamic revival movement in Malaysia since the mid-1970s. The Iranian Revolution of 1979 has given strength and succor to Islamic revivalism in Malaysia and elsewhere in the Muslim world. Signs of Islamic revivalism in Malaysia include the large numbers of Muslim women who cover their heads in public, the greater attention paid to religious ritual by Muslims, increased attendance during Friday prayers in the mosques, increased religious programming in the mass media, the commercial success of *nasyid* musical groups such as Raihan who sing religiously-inspired songs and so on. Although Islamic revival movements in Malaysia have generally been moderate in nature, it has resulted in some degree of uneasiness among Malaysians who are non-Muslims. This is because ethnic differences overlap with religious differences to a high degree in Malaysia, i.e., few Chinese are Muslims while Malays are overwhelmingly Muslim (there is also a relatively sizeable Indian Muslim population). Indeed, the Malaysian Constitution actually defines a "Malay" as a person who habitually speaks Malay, follows Malay customs and traditions and is a Muslim in religious belief. This official linking of ethnicity to religious orientation is unusual as compared to neighbouring nations like Indonesia where the native *Pribumi* ethnic groups can be Muslim, Hindu, Christian or whatever they wish to be. Unfortunately, "Muslim" religious extremist groups have appeared in Malaysia and have clashed with the government. This is a worrisome development because Islam in Malaysia has traditionally been moderate in its political orientation. One of the most notorious and shadowy groups is the Kesatuan Mujahideen Malaysia (KMM) which has been linked to Osama bin Laden and his extremist followers and sympathisers. Other groups are linked to the Jemaah Islamiah (JI) terrorist organisation in Indonesia. These extremist groups have been involved in terrorist bombings in Malaysia (relatively minor incidents), the Philippines and Indonesia (very serious with significant loss of life, i.e., the Bali incident and the bombing of an international-class hotel in Jakarta). In Malaysia, any attempt by extremist groups to link religion and ethnicity to anti-Establishment politics is kept under careful surveillance by the Malaysian police and its Special Branch (established to combat internal subversion and gangsterism). It is very likely that terrorist incidents in Malaysia have been relatively few and minor in severity because of the highly effective work being carried out behind the scenes by the police and its Special Branch.

Rightly or wrongly, the vast majority of non-Muslim Malaysians tend to regard PAS with a certain degree of suspicion since the ultimate aim of this political party is the establishment of an "Islamic state" in Malaysia. Thus, the gains made by PAS in the Malaysian general election of

1999 and the subsequent establishment of a PAS-led state government in the predominantly Malay state of Terengganu (in addition to its stronghold of Kelantan) was viewed with some degree of trepidation by the non-Muslim population of Malaysia. These feelings have not been alleviated by immoderate or controversial statements issuing forth from the mouths of certain high-level PAS leaders from time to time. To counter the growing influence of PAS, the Barisan Nasional has been implementing its own versions of Islamisation. Former Deputy Prime Minister Anwar Ibrahim played a major role in the formulation and implementation of these Islamisation policies beginning from the early 1990s until his abrupt removal from political office in September 1998.

The Anwar affair

This brings us next to one of the most controversial developments in recent Malaysian political history, i.e., the Anwar affair. Anwar, a charismatic individual, was a student leader while studying for his undergraduate degree in Malay Studies at Universiti Malaya. He was also a leader of the Angkatan Belia Islam Malaysia (ABIM) or the Islamic Youth Movement of Malaysia and was detained without trial for a number of years under the Internal Security Act during the 1970s. When he was recruited into UMNO in 1982, it was considered to be a great coup by the government since Anwar was also being courted by PAS. He rose rapidly in UMNO and in the Malaysian government. By 1993, he had become the Deputy Prime Minister. Anwar was widely regarded as the heir apparent to then Malaysian Prime Minister Dr Mahathir until he was ousted in late 1998 and subsequently arrested and charged with abuse of power and for allegedly committing "illegal" sexual acts. Apparently, Anwar was asked to resign as Deputy Prime Minister but he refused and was therefore sacked by Mahathir. Subsequently, he went up and down the country speaking at anti-government gatherings. He also used the premises of his official residence for anti-government rallies and finally, the government stepped in and arrested him. The Anwar affair resulted in unprecedented mass anti-government demonstrations in Kuala Lumpur. The Malaysian police was accused of excessive use of physical force in its handling of these demonstrations. The impartiality of the legal proceedings which led to Anwar's imprisonment have also been questioned. While in prison, Anwar was seriously beaten by an assailant who turned out to be none other than the then Inspector-General of Police. The Anwar affair is likely to be remembered as one of the most controversial incidents in Malaysian political history. This includes his sentencing for abuse of power and for sodomy (a criminal offense under Malaysian law). The Anwar affair has polarised the Malay population in Malaysia and rightly or wrongly, significant numbers of people continue to believe Anwar's assertions that he is innocent of all charges and that he was arrested, convicted and jailed simply because he was leading a *Reformasi* (Reform) movement and exposing corruption, cronyism and nepotism at the highest levels of the Malaysian political establishment. The curious thing, of course, is that he himself was part of this political establishment for many years prior to his arrest and imprisonment.

In the midst of the Anwar affair, a new political party called Parti Keadilan Nasional (National Justice Party, popularly referred to as "Keadilan") was formed and was made up of Anwar supporters who had quit UMNO, activists from local non-governmental organisations (NGOs) and certain dissident intellectuals. Anwar's wife, Dr Wan Azizah Wan Ismail, was elected to be one of the leaders of Keadilan. Keadilan made a respectable showing in the Malaysian general election of 1999 as a member of a loose coalition of opposition political parties made up of PAS, the Democratic Action Party (DAP) and Parti Rakyat Malaysia (PRM) (or the Malaysian People's Party). However, the primary beneficiary of this loose coalition was PAS which captured the state government of Terengganu (in addition to its traditional stronghold of Kelantan) and increased its number of parliamentary seats by a significant number. PAS also made significant gains in the heavily Malay northern states of Perlis and Kedah. The predominantly Chinese-based DAP was wracked by internal dissension over its informal cooperation with PAS while Keadilan was also affected by internal conflict and defections of members back to UMNO. Subsequently, the DAP left the opposition coalition because of its disagreement with PAS over the latter's aim of eventually establishing an "Islamic state" in Malaysia. Recently, Keadilan merged with the PRM in order to better oppose UMNO and the Barisan Nasional. However, in the Malaysian general election of 2004, Parti Keadilan Rakyat (the product of a merger between Keadilan and Parti Rakyat) performed poorly. As for the other major opposition parties, PAS lost control of the Terengganu state government while DAP did much better than in the 1999 general election.

Malaysia has a federal and state electoral system which, for historical reasons, is weighted in favour of the rural areas and at the expense of the urban areas. It is also weighted in favour of East Malaysia *vis-à-vis* West Malaysia. This system thus allows a smaller number of rural voters to elect one Member of Parliament as compared to the larger number of urban voters required for one MP. Similarly, relative to population size, Sabah and Sarawak send more MPs to the Malaysian Parliament as compared to the West Malaysian states. The result is that it allows political parties that are winning support in the rural areas such as PAS and political parties that are strong in East Malaysia such as the BN component parties to increase their representation in the Dewan Rakyat. Hence, UMNO and BN deem it very important to fight for the rural vote against PAS.

Recent developments
in Malaysian politics

New electronic media such as the Internet has affected Malaysian politics to a significant degree. The Anwar affair has resulted in a proliferation of pro-Anwar (and anti-Mahathir) websites. Opposition parties such as PAS and the DAP have also used the Internet to promote themselves and their ideologies and platforms. New electronic media means that the ruling Barisan Nasional government is losing its ability to control the mass media or silence opposition voices in Malaysia. This has certainly enlivened Malaysian politics.

A recent development in Malaysian politics is the establishment of the Human Rights Commission of Malaysia (Suruhanjaya Hak Asasi Manusia Malaysia or Suhakam). One of its more prominent members is Musa Hitam, a former Deputy Prime Minister of Malaysia. Musa served as Mahathir's first Deputy Prime Minister in the early 1980s. The establishment of Suhakam is viewed with scepticism (and even cynicism) by some members of the public while others view it with varying degrees of hope.

In recent years, various non-governmental organisations (NGOs) have emerged and are actively creating space for "civil society" in Malaysia. They work on women's issues, consumer issues, the environment and so on. Perhaps the best established of the NGOs are the Consumers Association of Penang (CAP) which publishes a respectable newspaper called the *Utusan Konsumer* and the Aliran social reform group which is also based in Penang. Feminist NGOs have been successful in raising awareness of important issues such as sexual harassment and domestic violence (in which women tend to be the main victims). Islamic feminist groups have also made their appearance, e.g., Sisters in Islam. Groups such as these argue that Islam and the promotion of greater rights for Muslim women are not incompatible. As Malaysia industrialises further and environmental conditions continue to deteriorate, the environmental NGOs are certain to intensify their activities in order to prod the authorities to take action and also to expose the activities of major polluters.

International relations

In terms of international politics and diplomacy, relations with neighbouring countries continue to be good with the occasional exceptions of Singapore and Australia. Relations with Singapore have always been prickly ever since the ouster of the city-state from the Federation of Malaysia after two short years of union (1963-1965). Some persistent issues between Malaysia and Singapore include the supply of cheap water from the state of Johor to Singapore, a territorial dispute over an island (called Pedra Branca by the Singaporeans and Pulau Batu Putih by the Malaysians), prime land in Singapore owned by KTM Bhd. (Malaysian Railways), the inability of West Malaysians to take out their Central Provident Fund (CPF) money—after quitting work in Singapore to return to Malaysia—until age 50, etc. Intemperate remarks by Singaporean Senior Minister Lee Kuan Yew about Johor as a place notorious for "muggings, shootings and carjackings" also contributed to problems in Malaysia-Singapore bilateral relations.

During Mahathir's tenure as Prime Minister, he showed strong signs of Malaysian nationalism and Third Worldism while continuing, pragmatically, to welcome foreign investment from the U.S., Western Europe, Japan and so on. Malaysia-Australia relations deteriorated during Mahathir's rule because of Australia's active role in supplying troops to protect East Timorese during East Timor's traumatic transition to independence from Indonesia. This was partly because of Mahathir's unsympathetic stand concerning separatist movements in Indonesia such as those in Aceh, Irian Jaya and East Timor. Whatever the case may be, an independent East Timor (renamed Timor Leste) is now a reality and its independence has been achieved after almost a quarter century of reportedly brutal invasion and occupation of this former Portuguese colony by the Indonesian armed forces. It will be interesting to see how the foreign policy of current Prime Minister Abdullah Ahmad Badawi (who once served as Malaysia's foreign minister) will differ from that of his predecessor.

Relations with other Southeast Asian nations such as Brunei, Thailand and the Philippines continue to be good although remarks made by the leaders of the latter two nations over the Anwar affair made the Malaysian government bristle. Malaysia has participated actively in political groupings of Islamic countries and also in regional or international groupings of Third World countries. Perhaps the only major area of concern when it comes to international relations is the Chinese military presence in the South China Sea. This is viewed with concern by Malaysia as well as by other Southeast Asian countries such as the Philippines. The South China Sea is a potential flashpoint in regional geopolitics as many nations have made territorial claims to the islands scattered over its surface (Vietnam and China have actually engaged in bloody military clashes over certain islands in the South China Sea). The presence of naval forces from other powers such as the U.S. further aggravate the situation.

Chapter 4

Economy

On attaining independence from Britain in 1957, the then Malayan economy was heavily reliant on agriculture and mining. The main exports (and earners of foreign exchange) were rubber and tin. Rubber had been introduced into colonial Malaya through seeds smuggled out from Brazil around the turn of the 20th century. As a result of the invention of the motorcar and its subsequent mass production by corporations like the Ford Motor Company in the U.S., the demand for natural rubber for making rubber tyres grew swiftly and rubber plantations blossomed all over Malaya. Malaya very quickly became the world's leading producer and exporter of rubber. As for tin, the main mining centres were located in the Kinta Valley around Ipoh and in the Klang Valley region. With the introduction of new technology such as the dredge, tin production increased greatly. These two industries led to strong demand for labour and thus, this demand was met by heavy immigration of people from the Indian subcontinent and from southern China. The export of rubber and tin also led to the growth of port cities such as Penang, Port Swettenham (now Port Klang) and Singapore. Other leading exports during the early days of Malaysia included timber and palm oil (Malaya became Malaysia in 1963 with the addition of the territories of British North Borneo, Sarawak and Singapore. Singapore left the federation in 1965 to become an independent nation.) Timber was extracted from the tropical rainforests of Peninsular Malaysia and from East Malaysia. Palm oil was extracted from the fruit of the oil palm tree which originated from West Africa. Besides workers in the rubber, tin, timber and palm oil industries, primary-sector workers included those engaged in padi cultivation and in fishing. Rice growing was and remains a major activity especially in states like Kedah and Kelantan. Later, petroleum and natural gas were discovered in the land or territorial waters offshore from Terengganu and Sarawak and thus, petroleum and natural gas production have become major economic activities in these two states.

The Malaysian authorities realised that if they did not industralise, Malaysia would remain subject to the mercy of continuously fluctuating prices of rubber, tin, timber and palm oil and would remain a relatively poor, primary commodity-producing Third World economy. Thus, import-substitution industries were first established and a few years later, Malaysia started encouraging investment by foreign multinational corporations in order to develop export-oriented industries in areas such as textiles and

electronics. Free Trade Zones (FTZs) or Export Processing
Zones (EPZs) were first set up in Penang and in the Klang
Valley near Sungei Way to facilitate foreign investment
from Japan, the U.S., Western Europe and other Asian
countries such as South Korea and Taiwan. After the
recession of the mid-1980s, accelerated effort was made to
attract foreign investors. This effort was successful (partly
because of rising labour costs and the appreciation of yen in
Japan) and today, Malaysia is a major exporter of industrial
products. Leading foreign investors include Singapore, the
U.S., Japan, Taiwan and nations from the European Union
such as Britain.

Labour shortages and immigration

Rapid industrialisation and high rates of economic growth
resulted in labour shortages. Thus, Malaysia started taking
in foreign workers from Indonesia, Bangladesh, the
Philippines, etc. Although economists like to talk of labour
as a "factor of production", in reality, we are dealing with
complex human beings. In good times, foreign workers are
a boon to the Malaysian economy. Foreign workers also do
the 3D jobs (dirty, difficult or dangerous) which Malaysians
tend to shun when the labour market is tight. However, in
times of economic recession, they would become a "social
problem" as unemployment rises in the work force.
Unemployed foreign workers would need to be dealt with
in a humane and ethical manner; it would be unfair to
simply deport them back to their home countries without
any form of financial or other assistance since they have
also contributed significantly to the growth of the
Malaysian economy.

Ordinary Malaysians typically encounter foreign workers in the form of male construction, plantation, timber or factory workers and female domestic, food service or janitorial workers. As with all immigrant groups that insert themselves into a foreign society at its lowest levels, negative stereotypes about them abound, e.g., they are blamed for contributing to higher crime rates and other social ills as well as for the proliferation of squalid "squatter" settlements in Malaysian cities and towns.

Foreign workers in Malaysia can be classified using the legal perspective (legal or illegal workers) or the human capital perspective (skilled or unskilled). Skilled, legal foreign workers would be a boon to any economy which is not in economic recession. Every effort should be made to attract these people (scientists, engineers, managers, financial experts, researchers, etc.) to join the labour force in Malaysia. Illegal, unskilled immigrant workers are a problem unless a situation of acute shortage of unskilled labour coupled with a booming economy occurs: because of their willingness to accept jobs at low wages, they will exert downward pressure on local wage rates. For this reason, the Malaysian Trades Union Congress (MTUC) is opposed to the intake of unskilled labour into the country. However, even if legal immigration of unskilled labour from neighbouring countries is discouraged, there are no effective means of preventing them from moving into the country illegally. This is indicated by the ease with which unskilled workers from Indonesia can slip into Malaysia.

Foreign workers are more than an abstract "factor of production". This is indicated by the social problems that can arise with the presence of foreign workers in Malaysia.

They have been accused of all sorts of things, e.g., contributing to crime and to the spread of slums in urban areas. Nevertheless, fair-minded Malaysians should be aware that they are highly vulnerable to victimisation—just like our poverty-stricken immigrant worker ancestors from China, India, Java, Sumatra, etc. during the colonial era. Foreign workers can be victimised at all stages of their odyssey from their respective countries of origin to Peninsular and East Malaysia. They are also vulnerable to abuse and exploitation after arrival. Those who victimise them include the people who smuggle them into Malaysia (often members of syndicates who make a lot of money from the smuggling of human beings), labour contractors, employers, and corrupt or brutal immigration and law enforcement officials both in their own country and in Malaysia. The more egregious cases of victimisation include the kidnapping or tricking of women into forced prostitution in Malaysia, debt slavery, non-payment of wages for extended periods of time, beatings and abuse of maids and other domestic workers (including physical, verbal, psychological and sexual abuse) and inhumane working hours and bad working conditions. In Malaysia, from time to time, one reads about cases of "maid abuse" in the mass media. There should be better protection of such people as they also contribute to Malaysia's economic progress by allowing Malaysian women to work outside the home. Filipino maids in Malaysia work six days a week and are allowed to take Sundays off. However, Indonesian maids have no day off and are supposed to work seven days a week. To make things even more unfair, they are paid less than the Filipino maids! There seems to be something morally wrong here. As for the treatment of illegal workers by the authorities, if proven to be true, alleged harsh conditions, malnutrition and ill-treatment in Malaysian detention camps established to house illegal migrant workers awaiting deportation can also be considered a form of abuse.

Competitive pressures

One major challenge that Malaysia faces as the structure of our economy changes (from an agricultural and mining economy to an exporter of manufactured goods with a significant service sector) is that we have to compete with other industrialising countries for foreign investment. Thus, we have to compete with neighbouring countries like Thailand, China and so on for investment from Western Europe, Japan, South Korea, Taiwan, Singapore and the U.S. As Malaysian wage levels rise, we will not be able to compete on the basis of low labour costs. Thus, other factors such as political stability, an efficient civil service, a highly developed system of transport and communications, and a skilled labour force are necessary in order to attract foreign investment.

Malaysia has become a major exporter of industrial goods. For example, we are one of the world's biggest exporters of air-conditioners. We are also a major player in the global microelectronics industry. Malaysia has also established an automobile industry (although only a small percentage of Malaysian-made cars are exported). However, all these industries continue to rely heavily on foreign technology and imported components. In order for us to make a successful transition to a dynamic, industrial economy and to higher value-added production, we need to develop local research and development (R&D) expertise and capability. We need to raise the skill level of the labour force as well as to train more managers, engineers and scientific researchers. In other words, access to post-secondary education needs to be broadened greatly. Malaysians should also be aware of the danger of technological or skill obsolescence and the necessity of lifelong learning and continuing education.

As mentioned earlier in the chapter on "Education", the higher education sector can also contribute to Malaysia's economic development through scientific and technological R&D. The research capability of Malaysian universities and other knowledge and technology-generating institutes needs to be enhanced and constantly improved upon. The number of scientific and industrial researchers is relatively low in relation to the population and the number of patents granted per year is also low. Malaysia needs to produce more scientific and industrial researchers, to stem emigration of Malaysian researchers and to encourage our researchers who are overseas to return home. The government can also allow and encourage private-sector corporations to actively recruit highly skilled foreigners to work in Malaysia. For example, if we want to develop a dynamic aerospace industry, we can recruit skilled labour from Russia since the Russian economy is experiencing serious problems and life is often very difficult for its people (including its scientific researchers). The countries of the world have been competing for foreign investment to increase their rates of economic growth. Increasingly, nations will have to compete for skilled and highly skilled labour to do so.

Forward-looking nations such as Singapore have been actively recruiting highly skilled professionals from the rest of Asia and beyond. The rationale is that highly skilled labour is a major contributor to economic growth; it is in limited supply domestically and therefore should be actively recruited from foreign countries to work in the city-state. In our opinion, this view is absolutely correct.

In Malaysia, development tends to be unbalanced geographically, i.e., most industrial activity tends to be concentrated in such areas as Penang and the Klang Valley. Areas such as Kelantan, Kedah, Perlis, Pahang and East Malaysia have not experienced much industrialisation and therefore, jobs are fewer and income levels are lower. This imbalance in regional development tends to encourage migration as people move to high-growth areas to seek jobs. High rates of economic growth in certain areas coupled with the in-migration it encourages can also give rise to problems: these include rising prices of housing, overburdened school systems, physical infrastructure that are stretched to the limit, traffic congestion and so on.

Privatisation

Malaysia has adopted the policy of "privatisation" since 1983. The term refers to the encouragement of private-sector involvement in industries or services that used to be provided by the government in the past. As the well-known social scientist Professor Jomo K.S. from the University of Malaya has pointed out, in Malaysia, "privatisation" can include any of the following:

- contracting out of services to the private sector, e.g., laundry services in public hospitals
- getting a private company to manage a public facility
- public-private joint ventures
- partial or total transfer of public facilities to the private sector
- allowing the private sector to build and operate schools, highways, etc.

Important services which have been privatised in Malaysia include telephone services, electricity supply and highways. Private-sector involvement in educational services has grown enormously. This is especially true in higher education. Large numbers of tertiary-level private colleges and universities exist and there are even branch campuses of foreign universities in Malaysia. Although the privatisation campaign was launched with the rationale that it would lower the financial burden of the government, increase efficiency and promote economic growth, some privatised entities have run into financial difficulties and have been "bailed out" or renationalised by the government. One of the most controversial examples of the latter was the rescue of Malaysia Airlines by the government through purchase of equity in the company (at a price significantly above the market price!). Another example, as mentioned by academician Dr Chan Chee Khoon of Universiti Sains Malaysia, is the privatisation of hospital support services such as cleansing services, linen and laundry services, facility engineering maintenance services, biomedical engineering maintenance services and clinical waste management services. Dr Chan has pointed out that after privatisation, the costs of these services to the government has risen from RM143 million in 1996 to RM468.5 million in 1997 (a three-fold increase after a year of privatisation) and to RM507.9 million in 1999. The question here is whether the improvements in service quality after privatisation are worth it in light of higher costs to the tax-payer.

Effects of globalisation

Malaysia has also been subjected to the forces of globalisation. Globalisation refers to the increasing economic as well as sociocultural integration of the nations of the world. Countries are increasingly tied together through international trade and flows of capital as well as flows of human beings. Economic globalisation was most spectacularly demonstrated by the rapid spread of the crisis that struck the Thai economy in July 1997 to other Asian countries such as South Korea, Malaysia and Indonesia. During the economic crisis, the Malaysian stock market fell drastically. The Malaysian ringgit was also subjected to speculative attacks by international currency traders and fell to almost RM5 to one U.S. dollar (the pre-crisis level was RM2.50=US$1). Fortunately, Malaysia weathered the economic crisis relatively well when compared to neighbouring Indonesia. The Malaysian government was bold enough to take unorthodox steps to fight the economic crisis. Although the Mahathir Administration was initially criticised and derided for its unorthodox response, we did avoid having to follow the dictates of the IMF and its so-called "structural adjustment programmes"

which have devastated neighbouring Indonesia and
brought about great suffering to its people. In fact, Nobel
Prize-winning economist Professor Joseph E. Stiglitz (who
was the Chief Economist at the World Bank during the
Asian financial crisis of the late 1990s) has roundly
condemned the IMF for its devastating policies in response
to the Asian Crisis and continues to do so in his important
books such as *Globalization and Its Discontents* (2002).
Concerned Malaysians are strongly encouraged to listen to
what Stiglitz has to say. In our opinion, if we had gone to
the IMF for aid and thus would have been forced to follow
the "conditionality" of its "structural adjustment
programmes", bankruptcies and unemployment would have
risen considerably, poorer citizens would have had much
reduced access to public services because of public
spending cutbacks and elimination of subsidies, inflation
would have accelerated because of currency devaluation,
etc. In other words, social distress would have increased
considerably because of the structural adjustment
programmes. Most likely, racial tension would also have
risen. Some people may continue to engage in academic
debates about whether Malaysia's unorthodox policies
actually "worked" in response to the financial crisis.
However, one of the authors of this book (who was trained
as a sociologist) would like to emphasise that we did
manage to avoid the human suffering created by IMF-style
programmes in the form of high unemployment, high
prices for basic necessities, physical attacks on ethnic
minorities, etc. in neighbouring countries such as Indonesia.

The countries of the world are also tied together
through flows of human beings, i.e., through labour

migration (skilled or unskilled and legal or illegal), students studying overseas, mass tourism and so on. In the sociocultural arena, globalisation would include the spread of values, beliefs, lifestyles and popular culture from one country to another. Malaysians who returned from overseas (especially those who have studied and worked for extended periods in foreign countries) are contributing greatly to economic development and social change in this country. For example, returned Malaysians have been active in the setting up of various non-governmental organisations (NGOs) dealing with the environment, women's rights and so on.

Protection of intellectual and other property rights

There is increasing recognition nowadays of the importance of protecting one's "intellectual property" such as trademarks, patents, technological secrets, etc. so as to derive or maintain a competitive advantage in the marketplace. Thus, the authorities need to take steps to actively protect Malaysia's intellectual property. Our "intellectual property" should be broadly defined to include indigenous technological knowledge such as knowledge of the healing properties of plants and herbs possessed by traditional *Orang Asli* and Malay healers, genetic material from living organisms in the Malaysian natural environment, etc. If we are not careful, unscrupulous foreigners will indulge in surreptitious collection of biological specimens and genetic material from Malaysia with the objective of obtaining potentially lucrative patents on these. As an example, there has actually been an attempt to patent traditional entities such as basmati rice, products from the neem tree, etc. (obtained from the Indian subcontinent) in the U.S.! Thus, the biological heritage and indigenous technological knowledge of less sophisticated Third World countries such as Malaysia is at risk of being patented for profit by individuals and commercial companies from the technologically advanced countries unless steps are taken to prevent this so-called "biopiracy".

Chapter 5

Race and Ethnicity

MALAYSIA is a multiracial, multiethnic nation. This is
nothing unusual for a Third World nation which is an
ex-colony of the European imperial powers. Most of the
nations of the Third World are "accidents of history", i.e.,
they are the direct descendants of colonies carved out in a
haphazard manner by the Europeans during the heyday of
colonialism and imperialism. The major imperial powers
such as Portugal, Spain, Belgium, Holland, Germany, Italy,
Britain and France divided up the Americas, the Caribbean,
Africa, Asia and Oceania between themselves without
rhyme or reason. (Other imperial powers such as Russia,
Japan and Turkey in the form of the Ottoman Empire were
also involved in the "scramble for empire".) Sometimes,
arbitrary boundaries were drawn between their colonies
and this either divided up a single ethnic group between
different colonies or mixed up tens or even hundreds of

ethnic groups within the boundaries of a single colony. Colonial powers also encouraged mass immigration to obtain labour power for agricultural plantations, extraction of mineral resources, building of railroads and so on. Mass immigration made the composition of colonial populations even more complex. The best examples of contemporary Third World nations with hundreds of ethnic groups within their boundaries are the Democratic Republic of the Congo (formerly called Zaire) in Central Africa and the Republic of Indonesia. The Belgians carved out a huge colony in the middle of Africa and the Dutch created the "Dutch East Indies" out of thousands of widely scattered islands in Southeast Asia. When these colonies became independent, their new rulers were faced with the headache of trying to create a sense of unity and common identity out of hundreds of ethnic groups with their own distinct languages, religions, customs and traditions and so on.

Modern "Malaysia" comprises territories once ruled or dominated by the British such as Malaya, British North Borneo (now known as Sabah) and Sarawak. Singapore was also part of Malaysia from 1963-1965. During the days of British rule, large numbers of people migrated to Malaya, British North Borneo and Sarawak from southern China. Similarly, large numbers of people were recruited from the Indian subcontinent to work in Malaya. There was also immigration from Sumatra, Java and so on. All these, coupled with heterogeneity of the indigenous peoples in East Malaysia, have resulted in an independent Malaysia with many tongues, creeds and colours. This has made "nation-building" more difficult and challenging.

The social construction of race and ethnicity and changes in ethnic definitions over time

Most people in Malaysia view ethnicity as something that is biological in origin. Social scientists, on the other hand, view ethnicity as a "social construction", i.e., it is man-made and ethnic identity can emerge, change over time and even disappear completely! It can also be imposed by a politically dominant group on other politically subordinated groups. For example, Malaysians whose ancestors came from South Asia are actually a very heterogenous lot. They may be Bengali, Tamil, Singhalese, Malayalee, Gujarati, Punjabi, Sindhi, Pushtun, etc. They may also be Muslim, Hindu, Buddhist, Christian, Sikh or Jain. Yet, all of them were labelled as "Indian" by the British colonial authorities and this ethnic label has been passed on to their descendants in contemporary Malaysia. The so-called *Orang Asli* of Peninsular Malaysia is another good example of different ethnic groups that have had a generic label imposed on them.

The "Chinese" in Malaysia are equally heterogenous. They are descendants of immigrants from different areas of South China and speak different dialects such as Hokkien, Cantonese, Teochew, Hainanese, Hakka, Hokchiu, Henghua, etc. These dialects are often mutually unintelligible. In Kuala Lumpur, Ipoh, Seremban, and in towns in Pahang, the common Chinese dialect is Cantonese. Members from all the different dialect groups can speak Cantonese if they grew up in these towns and cities. In towns like Penang, Melaka, Kuala Terengganu, etc. the common dialect is Hokkien. Thus a Chinese person from Penang who cannot speak Cantonese but who works in Kuala Lumpur may have to resort to the use of English or Mandarin Chinese to communicate with the local Chinese. There is also a group of "Chinese" called the *Peranakans* (or Straits Chinese) that emerged in Penang, Melaka and Singapore during the colonial days. They are the descendants of intermarriages between Chinese immigrant men and local native women. Often, they cannot speak Mandarin or any of the Chinese dialects: they only speak English or a Malay patois in their homes. Today, the Peranakan are undergoing "re-sinicization" and are merging back into the "Chinese" mainstream, i.e., Peranakan identity is gradually weakening or even disappearing. In the past there was tension between Mandarin-educated and English-educated Chinese. There was even "racial tension" between some of the Chinese dialect groups (such as the Cantonese and the Hakka) but all these no longer exist and "intermarriage" between the different Chinese dialect groups is very extensive today.

The emergence of a pan-Malaysian "Chinese" identity out of these various dialect groups has been attributed to factors such as the usage of Mandarin Chinese as the language of instruction (Mandarin Chinese is actually a Northern Chinese dialect foreign to the Southern Chinese) in schools, the herding of Chinese who lived on jungle fringes into "New Villages" during the Emergency of 1948-1960 in order to cut off Communist insurgents from their supporters, political mobilisation along ethnic lines, and to government policies that inadvertently reinforce ethnic identity such as "affirmative action" programmes (or preferential policies) based on ethnicity. Today, 90 per cent of Malaysian Chinese kids start their formal educational career in primary schools (both private and public) that use Mandarin Chinese as the main language of instruction. Thus, although many of them will move on to Malay-language public-sector secondary schools later on, this early start also helps to create a sense of "Chinese" identity.

The "Malays" in Malaysia are also by no means homogenous. Some Malaysian Malays are descendants of Bugis immigrants from modern-day Sulawesi in Indonesia. Others are descendants of immigrants from Minangkabau and Mandailing areas in Sumatra or descendants of immigrants from Java. The Minangkabau influence is evident in the architecture and customs of the Malays of Negri Sembilan. There are also many kampungs called "Kampung Jawa" (i.e., Java Village) in Malaysia. Regional identities such as those found among the Kelantan Malays also continue to exist. Another phenomenon contributing to heterogeneity among the Malays is intermarriage between a Malay and a non-Malay (such as a Chinese or Indian) where the children produced by the intermarriage are brought up as Malays and consider themselves (and are considered by others) to be Malays. When a non-Muslim marries a Muslim in Malaysia, the non-Muslim is expected to convert to Islam and to adopt a Muslim name. Since the Muslims in Malaysia are mostly Malays (there are some Indian Muslims but very few Chinese Muslims), this facilitates the adoption of a Malay-Muslim identity especially among the children produced by such marriage. Therefore, a "Malay" in Malaysia may have Orang Asli, Chinese, Indian, Middle Eastern, Caucasian or other forebears among his ancestors even if a common "Malay" ethnic identity has emerged in contemporary Malaysia. For example, Mahathir's paternal grandfather is a Malayalee from Kerala in India while Abdullah Ahmad Badawi's maternal grandfather is a Chinese Muslim from Hainan Island in China. Furthermore, Abdullah's wife has a Japanese mother. Similarly, former Prime Minister Tunku Abdul Rahman's mother was Thai while another former Prime Minister Hussein Onn had Turkish ancestors.

An *Orang Asli* identity has been created in West Malaysia from the different groups of nomadic hunter-gatherers and settled villagers. Those who retain their animist religious beliefs will continue to remain distinct from Malay-Muslims while those who convert to Islam are likely to merge into the Malay-Muslim community. As for East Malaysia, the extreme heterogeneity of the indigenous peoples (Iban, Bidayuh, Melanau, Kayan, Kenyah, Kadazan, Murut, Penan, etc.) means that many ethnic identities exist. Those who are Muslim such as some of the Melanau (there are also Melanau who are Christians) may eventually come to be regarded as Malays but like the *Orang Asli*, those who are animist or Christian will maintain separate identities.

Bangsa Malaysia

Although former Malaysian Prime Minister Dr Mahathir expressed hopes for the emergence of a *"Bangsa Malaysia"* or "Malaysian Race", this is unlikely to occur for the foreseeable future. Especially in West Malaysia, the barriers to intermarriage and a thorough mixing of the different ethnic groups are many and difficult to surmount. One major barrier is the religious barrier. Malaysians who are Muslim can intermarry with each other relatively easily, e.g., intermarriage between Malays and Indian Muslims. However, as mentioned earlier, intermarriage between two people who come from a Muslim and a non-Muslim background is difficult because the social situation in Malaysia requires the non-Muslim partner to convert to Islam. Thus, intermarriage between the major ethnic groups such as that between Malays and Chinese is likely to remain low. There are more interethnic marriages in East Malaysia (for e.g., between Chinese and Kadazan) in the state of Sabah.

Importance of careful management of ethnic tensions

Relatively high rates of economic growth and preferential policies based on ethnicity have reduced economic inequality between the Malays and the Chinese. This has reduced overt ethnic tension to some extent. Nevertheless, the maintenance of tranquil interethnic relations will remain a major challenge for all Malaysians of goodwill for the foreseeable future.

Viewing Malaysia's ethnic diversity as a plus factor

It is much better to view Malaysia's ethnic diversity as a boon rather than as a "problem". Ethnic diversity makes the sociocultural landscape varied and much more interesting. Malaysian cuisine, for instance, is all the more richer and interesting because of the many different ethnic groups that comprise the population. One only needs to look at the cooking of the *Peranakan* or Straits Chinese to illustrate this point. The different ethnic groups have borrowed from the culture (and cuisine) of each other and this has made the Malaysian *rojak* society much more fascinating and enriching. Thus, foreign tourists find Malaysia fascinating because of our heterogeneous population with its diverse festivals, customs and traditions. Multiculturalism coupled with tolerance of and respect for differing worldviews, beliefs, lifestyles, etc. also make it easier for Malaysians to face the challenges of globalisation in its various aspects, for e.g., it gives us a competitive advantage when we do business in China, Taiwan, India and other South Asian countries, Indonesia or Western countries.

Chapter 6

Transport, Communications and the Mass Media

On independence in 1957, Malaya had a relatively good system of transport and communications. The road system was quite extensive (even if the main highways were mostly two-lane) and the inter-city rail system was quite well developed. The country was also well served by major ports such as Penang and Port Swettenham (now called Port Klang). With the formation of Malaysia in 1963, the major port of Singapore became part of national territory. However, transportation linkages between the west and east coasts of Peninsular Malaysia were few in number. There were essentially only two major roads from west to east, i.e., the road to Kota Baru via Gua Musang in Kelantan and the road to Kuantan via Temerloh in Pahang. Another road was from Johor Baru to Kuantan via Mersing on the east coast of Johor and Pahang states. During the northeast monsoon season, travel from Kuala Lumpur to Kuantan could cease completely because of floods along the way. Even during normal times, travel was not smooth because of the large number of timber lorries on the road, the slow ferry connection at the Pahang River at Temerloh, and the narrow, winding road going up and down the Main Range mountains at Bentong. In the East Malaysian states of Sabah and Sarawak, the situation was much worse. Partly because of the large size of the two states, their thickly forested interior, small populations, neglect by the colonial authorities and so on, their transport and communication systems were seriously underdeveloped and lacking.

Today, after more than four decades of independence from British colonial rule, the Malaysian transport and communication system has been greatly improved. Although the port of Singapore has been "lost" since Singapore left the Federation and became a sovereign nation in 1965, Malaysian exporters continue to ship a significant amount of products to other nations through the port of Singapore. New ports have been built near Kuantan in Pahang and at Pasir Gudang to the east of Johor Baru. Recently, another port was built at Tanjung Pelepas near Johor Baru. A major four-lane highway called the North-South Highway (Projek Lebuhraya Utara-Selatan) was constructed in West Malaysia in the early 1990s. It connects Johor Baru at the extreme southern end of the peninsula to Bukit Kayu Hitam in Northern Kedah and into Thailand itself. A likely reason why the North-South Highway sweeps into Northern Kedah rather than into Kangar and the rest of Perlis is because Bukit Kayu Hitam lies within the Kubang Pasu electoral district of former Prime Minister Dr Mahathir Mohamad. An East-West

highway has also been built to connect Grik in Kedah to
northern Kelantan and Kota Baru. Another highway which
has facilitated travel is the Segamat-Kuantan highway
which serves as an alternative to the Johor Baru-Kuantan
highway via Mersing and Rompin. As for the road from
Kuantan to Kuala Lumpur, improvements such as the
bridge over the Pahang River at Temerloh, the tunnel at the
Pahang-Selangor border and the Kuala Lumpur-Karak
highway have made travel somewhat smoother. The road
system in East Malaysia has also been much improved
although travel by boat and air remains important.

Although the North-South Highway and other similar
highways have made travel times between many towns in
West Malaysia significantly shorter, toll charges are rather
high. In the past, travel by road between cities such as
Penang and Kuala Lumpur was "free". Nowadays, motorists
have to pay out large sums in toll money. Sometimes, travel
times can even be made longer by traffic jams formed by
cars exiting or entering large cities such as Kuala Lumpur.
For example, in the late 1960s, travel time between Kuala
Lumpur and the town of Kuantan on the East Coast of
Peninsular Malaysia was about 4.5 hours. Today, in spite of
the existence of the Kuala Lumpur-Karak Highway (which
has eliminated the need to negotiate the treacherously
winding Bentong road over the mountains) and a higher
speed limit from Karak to Kuantan, total driving time
remains at about 4.5 hours! The reason for this is because it
takes much longer to get out of and into the Kuala Lumpur
metropolitan area because of traffic jams. A case of two
steps forward and two steps back indeed. The stretch of the
North-South Highway between Tapah and Kuala Lumpur

in the north (and Seremban and Kuala Lumpur in the south) is also notorious for traffic jams at the end of long weekends and holidays when people are travelling back to Kuala Lumpur for school and work.

Traffic congestion and traffic jams are getting worse and worse in Malaysian towns and cities because of rising income levels, the appearance of local car manufacturers heavily protected by tariffs such as Proton and Perodua, and lack of political commitment to the development of efficient public transportation systems. As income levels rise, cars become more affordable. Furthermore, the number of cars owned by each family also rises. The introduction of low-priced, locally-produced mini-cars such as the "Kancil" has allowed some people to "upgrade" from the motorcycle. In contrast to countries like Singapore and the Netherlands that have realised that the policy of building more and more roads will never solve the problem of worsening traffic jams, Malaysia continues to pave over more and more of its city environs and countryside with highways. It has been estimated in the U.S. that motor vehicles contribute as much as 50 per cent to air pollution in American cities. If Malaysia does not take action to avoid being a "car and highway-dependent" nation, the air quality in our cities and towns can only get worse and worse. Furthermore, unless the public authorities encourage the development of alternatives such as efficient and cheap mass transport systems, the number of motor vehicles on the road will only get bigger and bigger and traffic jams will only get worse and worse. In countries like the Netherlands and Japan, people ride bicycles or take the train a lot. Bicycles are an efficient and "environmentally-friendly" (as well as healthy) form of transportation for small towns and even for short trips in large cities. An example of the latter is the presence of cyclists even in gigantic cities like Tokyo in Japan. However, bicycle lanes need to be created in order to make cycling in Malaysian towns and cities safe.

Railway service in Malaysia also needs to be made more extensive and effective. This also applies to rail service within large cities in the form of "light rail" systems. If commuter rail, light rail and monorail services are well developed and priced reasonably, it is likely that many motorists would take the train rather than drive into cities like Kuala Lumpur and Penang from the surrounding suburbs.

Singapore is one of Malaysia's leading trading partners. However, it seems to us that there is plenty of room for improvement with respect to the road and rail links between the two countries. One example is the massive traffic jams and delays that one often sees at the Causeway linking Johor Baru and Woodlands in northern Singapore. The need for a replacement for the Causeway is evident. One also sees large numbers of people queuing up for buses to take them between Malaysia and Singapore. We wonder if the Singapore and Malaysian governments have ever considered the possibility of building a rapid, fully automatic shuttle train to take passengers between Johor Baru and Woodlands?

There is also the second link between Gelang Patah in Johor and Tuas in Singapore. However, this Link is underutilised because of the greater distance as compared to the Woodlands link and also because of the high toll charges.

In order to reduce travel time between Kuala Lumpur and Singapore, commercial travellers often fly by taking the air shuttle service provided by Malaysia Airlines and Singapore Airlines. Although the actual flight takes less than an hour, if one adds in the time taken to travel to and from the respective airports, the time spent waiting for the flight and so on, total travel time saved may not amount to much compared to travel by road. One solution to this is to build a high speed rail link between Kuala Lumpur and Singapore. The famous Shinkansen "bullet trains" of Japan and high-speed TGV trains of France can be used as models in the design of such a system. Similarly, high speed rail links can also be built to connect major cities and towns in Malaysia, e.g., between Penang and Kuala Lumpur, Ipoh and Kuala Lumpur, etc.

Air travel between Peninsular Malaysia and East Malaysia is relatively expensive and lengthy when the time taken to get to and from the airport, waiting time, etc. are factored in. Can a high speed ferry service (using hydrofoils) be introduced to make travel between Johor and Sarawak easier?

Alternatively, the appearance of more "cut rate" airlines like Air Asia can be encouraged by the government in order to increase price competition and facilitate air travel between Peninsular Malaysia and East Malaysia. Malaysian transport policy needs to be driven more by economic logic and efficiency considerations rather than by politics and rent-seeking behaviour. For example, it is curious why the popular and well-located Subang Airport was closed down and domestic travellers were forced to make the "great trek" to the Kuala Lumpur International Airport (KLIA) in Sepang when this not only made it more expensive but also increased inconvenience and travel time for the domestic travellers.

The Malaysian mass media

The mass media in Malaysia can be divided into "traditional mass media" and "new mass media". Traditional mass media would include things like printed matter, radio, television and movies. Newer forms of communication and mass media would include the fax, video compact discs, cellular phones and the Internet. In the past, there were no private radio and television stations. Today, the government has allowed private TV stations to be established, e.g., TV3, NTV7 and 8TV (previously known as Metrovision).

Unlike the free-wheeling press in Western countries like the U.S., Malaysia's mass media is heavily regulated by the government. Furthermore, many of the newspapers and TV stations are also owned or controlled by political parties from the ruling Barisan Nasional. Malaysia therefore does not have a free press in the Western sense. The government argues that this is necessary in order to preserve ethnic and religious harmony but critics definitely "beg to differ". However, with the appearance of new technologies such as the World Wide Web (popularly called the "Internet"), alternative media have proliferated. Websites critical of the government such as *Free Malaysia* and *Malaysia Kini* have made their appearance. Pro-Anwar Ibrahim websites also sprung up in significant numbers after he was arrested by the police. Technological advances such as the Internet have made censorship of the mass media harder and harder for the public authorities to maintain.

Traditionally, the Malaysian government has also subjected foreign TV programmes and movies to censorship, e.g., censorship of sex and violence. However, again because of advances in technology such as the Internet and the appearance of videotapes and compact discs, censorship has become increasingly difficult to carry out. Prior to the crackdown on video piracy, uncensored movies in the form of videotapes and video compact discs were easily available from hawkers at Malaysia's ubiquitous *pasar malam*. Sexually explicit material are also easily accessible on the Internet. Thus, parents may need to install "Cybernanny software" to make it harder for their children to access certain kinds of websites and the government should also seriously consider introducing effective sex education in schools in order to promote responsible sexual behaviour among adolescents. This is easier said than done of course because of religious sensibilities in Malaysia, e.g., an attempt by the Ministry of Education to conduct a sex survey in Malaysian public schools was aborted in the face of strong opposition from conservative Muslim clergy and laity.

The Malaysian government's grand plan to promote a K-economy (Knowledge Economy) through the launching of the Multimedia Super Corridor (MSC) project also makes it harder to regulate Internet access and Internet content. Indeed, the Malaysian government has actually declared that there would not be any censorship of the Internet so as not to discourage foreign investment in the MSC. Whatever the case may be, the explosive growth of the Internet in recent years is a clear case of technological advances outpacing the adaptive ability of social and cultural institutions (the so-called "sociocultural lag" problem).

Nowadays, cellular phones are becoming more and more common in Malaysia. To facilitate cellphone communications, transmission towers are sprouting up all over the place (including on the roofs of shophouses and other commercial buildings). The increased use of cellphones and the proliferation of transmission towers have given rise to concerns about their possible effects on health. There is not only a potential health hazard, there is also the question of aesthetics. These transmission towers should be properly regulated in order to protect the health of the public and to prevent further "uglification" of the cities, towns and countryside.

Chapter 7

Housing and Environment

THE Malaysian countryside used to be a "green" countryside (albeit a lot of the greenery was due to seemingly endless stands of oil palm or rubber trees). However, these days, the "concrete jungle" is spreading as a result of highway construction, urban sprawl as more and more housing estates are built on the outskirts of cities and towns, the setting up of industrial estates and so on. As the network of highways and roads spreads across the length and breadth of the countryside, the jungle and plantations surrounding the roads are subsequently cut down and replaced with houses, commercial buildings and factories. It is actually quite pathetic to see large and luxuriant trees cut down to be replaced with skinny-looking "ornamental" trees with sparse foliage that provide minimal shade to travellers who stop for one reason or another. We must keep in mind that the Malaysian jungle is rich in natural resources: jungle plants can be a source of new pharmaceutical drugs and the genetic material found in the jungle are increasingly valuable as the biotechnology industry grows in importance in the 21st century. Steps have been taken to tackle the problem of biopiracy by passing relevant laws. (Biopiracy refers to individuals and corporations from more technologically advanced nations collecting or even stealing genetic and biological material from developing nations and patenting them for commercial gain and without proper compensation to the developing nations.) If we do not actively protect our natural resources from destruction by our own hands, what is the use of passing more and more biopiracy laws? One way to protect the Malaysian jungle is to create more national parks and to promote "ecotourism". Ecotourism is attractive to citizens from highly urbanised countries like Singapore that lack greenery and to people from Western countries who may want to travel to Malaysia to escape from the winter season.

Urban sprawl, rural-to-urban migration and squatter settlements

A good example of destruction of the natural environment through urban sprawl and growth of the "concrete jungle" is the "development" of the Klang Valley whereby one finds it increasingly difficult to tell where one municipality ends and the next begins, e.g., it is getting difficult to tell where Kuala Lumpur ends and Petaling Jaya begins, where Petaling Jaya ends and Subang Jaya begins, where Subang Jaya ends and Shah Alam begins and so on all the way down to Klang and Port Klang. If this process of urban sprawl continues unabated, "development" would threaten to become "uglification" (from the word "ugly") and "land scarification" (from the word "scar") instead!

There are winners and losers from this physical phenomenon known as urban sprawl. The winners include real estate developers and rural or suburban land owners whose land increase in market value. Losers include nomadic *Orang Asli* and other tribal people whose habitats shrink and rubber and oil palm plantation workers who lose their jobs and their housing (when plantations are cut down to be replaced by factories, commercial buildings, housing estates, and even golf courses and theme parks!) Displaced rubber and oil palm workers often have no choice but to migrate to the cities and towns and settle down in squalid "squatter" areas. These squatter areas are hotbeds of unemployment, underemployment, crime and other social problems. In fact, some Malaysian social scientists believe that the increasing social problems found in the Indian community may be due to the involuntary displacement of Indian estate workers through this process.

Housing in Malaysia

The positive side of the increase in the number of housing estates is that the Malaysian population is becoming better housed over time, i.e., living space per person is increasing as houses become bigger (such as two-storey buildings replacing single-storey buildings) while parents have fewer children at the same time. The quality of houses that are being built has also become better over time (more attractive in design, more toilets and bathrooms per house, etc.). Some Malaysians prefer living in the so-called "condominiums" instead of houses. Although these are highrise and high-density housing, they like the amenities that go with condominium living, e.g., swimming pools, tennis courts, gyms, club facilities, etc. in the condominium complex.

Middle-class and upper-class Malaysians are living in better and better quality housing. However, significant numbers of lower class Malaysians live in relatively small, highrise flats while the poorest Malaysians live in unsightly and unhealthy squatter settlements in the urban areas or ramshackle housing without proper water supply and sanitation in the rural areas. Furthermore, it has been reported that some rubber and oil palm estate owners provide their workers with substandard housing or inadequate water supply, toilet and sanitation services. Thus, the Malaysian government needs to take action to make better quality low-cost housing more available and affordable to Malaysians from the lower classes.

Our Malaysian architects should also try to design buildings that look more "Asian" in general and "Malaysian" in particular. If they just mindlessly copy design trends from the West (such as the "International Style" in the past and "Post-Modern" at the present), Malaysian cities such as Kuala Lumpur will not look any different from cities in Western countries. Why would foreign tourists from Western countries fly in to visit Kuala Lumpur if it looks just like Auckland, Sydney, London or Los Angeles? We need to preserve not only historical sites but also high-quality buildings constructed during the colonial era and the first few decades of independence. These sites and buildings would not only help to remind us about our past but would also help to enhance the attractiveness of Malaysia to foreign tourists. The façade of buildings from the colonial era and first few decades of independence can be preserved even if the building is used as a restaurant, shop or other commercial building.

Air and cross-border pollution

As Malaysia undergoes rapid industrialisation, the environment is being affected adversely. Air, water and solid waste pollution are becoming significant problems. Some have also argued that the disappearance of jungle in the interior and mangrove swamps along the coasts are also cause for concern.

A major cause of air pollution in cities and towns is the increasing number of motor vehicles. Another reason is the increase in the number of factories. Possible solutions to the problem of air pollution include better public transport such as light-rail systems within towns and high-speed rail between towns, more stringent standards and strong enforcement of standards for motor vehicle emissions (the sight of motorcycles spewing out smoke and lorries and buses spewing out even thicker and blacker smoke never ceases to distress us!) There should also be stronger enforcement of anti-pollution laws in order to control pollution by factories. Beginning in the early 1990s, the problem of "cross-border pollution" emerged, i.e., the infamous "haze" drifting into Peninsular Malaysia from Sumatra and into East Malaysia from Kalimantan. Some people believe that Malaysian plantation companies operating in Indonesia are also contributing to the haze by practising irresponsible open burning in order to clear land for cultivation of oil palm trees cheaply.

Water pollution and water shortage

Another environmental problem in Malaysia is water pollution. Many rivers in Malaysia are significantly polluted. Polluted rivers are not only unsightly (and sometimes offensive to human noses), they can also be health or even fire hazards since oily material floating on rivers can actually catch fire! A related problem is deforestation upstream that destroys water catchment areas resulting in flash floods, pollution of rivers downstream with mud and other debris, and even water shortages. The deforestation can be due to logging activities or to the construction of roads and buildings such as condominiums in hilly areas. The collapse of the "Highland Towers" condominiums in the Kuala Lumpur metropolitan area is the most notorious example of reckless housing construction on hill slopes. Deforestation in the Cameron Highlands region has resulted in the silting of bodies of water and possibly even modified the local climate. Pollution of streams and rivers will also affect the seas surrounding Malaysia and affect the tourist industry negatively.

Solid waste pollution and inadequate green consciousness among Malaysians

Yet another problem is solid waste pollution. Malaysia is becoming more and more a wasteful "throwaway society" every day. Unless "Green consciousness" grows among our people, we will continue to generate more and more solid waste in the years ahead. Green consciousness would include awareness of the problem of environmental deterioration and the taking of active steps to fight this problem, e.g., generating less solid waste, reusing and recycling of material, etc. In Malaysia, there is active recycling of newsprint. However, other than that, recycling of other material is not much in evidence. We Malaysians can learn a lot from the Japanese in terms of control of the solid waste pollution problem. We should also be mindful of the problem of e-waste, i.e., solid waste in the form of discarded computer and electronics equipment. Such waste is a serious problem because it contains toxic material that are hazardous to health. The ever shortening product life cycles of computer and electronics equipment can only compound the e-waste problem. Currently, solid waste is either buried in landfills or incinerated. Such processing of solid waste can also give rise to other forms of pollution, i.e., water pollution if material in the waste leaks into underground aquifers or streams or rivers and air pollution if the incinerated material gives off ashes and toxic gases.

Chapter 8

Culture and Religion

AMONG all living organisms, human beings are unusual in that we have highly developed systems of norms (culturally-specific ideas of what is "acceptable behaviour" and what is "unacceptable behaviour"), values and beliefs, rituals, etc. which can be called by the term "culture". Although other primates like chimpanzees and gorillas exhibit the rudiments of culture, our linguistic ability and our great intelligence allows us to invent new things and to pass them on efficiently to later generations in the form of oral traditions and more importantly, through writing. Cultural exchange between human groups and societies are ongoing—there is no human society which has not borrowed ideas and tools from other societies. Thus, the cultures of the various ethnic groups in Malaysia are constantly evolving and part of this evolution is due to the influence of the other ethnic groups. Thus, the cuisine of the Chinese in Malaysia has been influenced by Malay and Indian cuisine. In turn, Malay and Indian cuisine show the signs of the influence of Chinese cuisine and so on.

This is also the case with the Malaysian vernacular languages. We have borrowed from each other and come up with interesting new combinations of words and expressions. For example, Chinese dialects such as Cantonese have incorporated Malay words like *"pasar"* (pronounced *"pak sat"*), *longkang, pandai* (pronounced *"pa nai"*), *semua* (pronounced *"som mah"*), etc. Thus, when a Malaysian speaks the local version of Cantonese, a Hong Kong Chinese may find our Cantonese strange, amusing or even alarming! Malay itself has many Indian loan words such as *tali, raja, roti* and so on. This is not surprising as Malay societies were strongly influenced by Indian culture before the spread of Islam to this part of the world. This is evident from court rituals in Malaysian states which have Sultans and from places like Bali in Indonesia which somehow were never converted to Islam. English, the language of the former colonial power, has also influenced all the Malaysian vernacular languages to a significant extent. In turn, the English language in Malaysia has evolved into a particular variant which sounds very strange to British and American ears called Malaysian English or "Manglish" (Mangled English?).

One of the most famous Manglish additions is, of course, the word *"lah"*. The word *"lah"* is a multifunctional word! It can be used for emphasis (as in "No-*lah*!"), to express anxiety ("Die-*lah*"), to soften refusals to requests for help ("Cannot-*lah*"), to express impatience ("Hurry up-*lah*!") and so on. This author remembers reading about a member of the Beatles who used the word *"lah"* when he was being interviewed by a member of the British mass media. This resulted in great bewilderment on the part of the latter! There is also the strange use of the word "one" in Manglish, e.g., as in "My one", "Your one", "You so bad one!", etc. Sometimes, Manglish expressions are direct translations from Malaysian vernacular languages such as Malay, e.g., "shake leg" (from the Malay *goyang kaki*, meaning to take things easy) and "where got?" (from the Malay *mana ada*) or Cantonese, e.g., "You never tell me how I know?" Personally speaking, we feel that although we should learn to speak and write Standard English when dealing with foreigners and when we are in formal situations, Manglish should not be denigrated but should be considered an integral and living part of Malaysian society and culture. It is also great fun! For example, the close cousin of Manglish called Singlish (Singapore English) has been used to great and humorous effect in the popular TV series called *Phua Chu Kang* in Singapore. To quote Phua Chu Kang (no relation to one of this book's authors), "PCK Private Limited. Best in Singapore, JB and some say ....". If this is transcribed into Standard English, it loses much of its punch indeed.

The way that Malaysians dress is also the result of cultural interchange. For example, the Chinese and Indians have largely adopted "Western dress" for everyday wear while Malay males dress mostly in Western style for everyday wear but not for other occasions such as going to the mosque for Friday prayers, etc. On the other hand, Malay females increasingly dress in "Islamic-Malay style" as a result of the revivalism of Islam in the country. The majority of Muslim women cover their heads in public whereas this was not the case thirty years ago. On the other hand, Chinese and Indian clothes like the *samfoo* and the *saree* are slowly disappearing since few young Chinese and Indian females dress in these styles nowadays. However, Chinese teenagers who are influenced by pop stars, actors and actresses from Hong Kong, Taiwan or Japan may dress in styles that cause consternation among their elders, e.g., dyeing their hair yellow, dressing in black clothes from head to toe (black is an unlucky colour reserved for sad occasions such as funerals among the Chinese) and so on.

As a result of Western influence spread by English-language education, the mass media, study abroad in Western countries, etc., the behaviour of young Malaysians can be very different from that of their elders. Thus, higher rates of smoking and drinking among non-Muslim Malaysian females often bring clucks of disapproval from the older generations. Sexual behaviour has also changed among young Malaysians. Premarital sex and even cohabitation—behaviour once strongly frowned upon—are occuring among the non-Muslim young in the big cities.

Islamic revivalism in Malaysia

Islamic revivalism is a recent development among Malays and other Muslims in Malaysia. Islamic revivalism first emerged in the late 1960s and then gathered strength with the appearance of the Iranian Revolution in 1979. Islamic revivalism has profoundly changed Malay society in Malaysia. More and more religious schools (including private ones) have also sprung up in Malaysia. This religious revivalism has, rightly or wrongly, given rise to feelings of apprehension among non-Muslim Malaysians and even among more secular Malays. Things are not helped by periodic eyebrow-raising pronouncements from the conservative male leadership of PAS or by the appearance of religious extremist groups that claim to be "Islamic" in orientation. Attendance of Muslim males at Friday prayers is up and there are also other signs of increased religiosity such as more religious programmes in the mass media, bestselling *nasyid* musical groups and so on.

Islamic revivalism is a complex phenomenon in Malaysia. Some versions of revivalism are stricter than other versions and this can give rise to controversy, e.g., groups such as Al-Arqam have been officially declared as "deviant" cults and have been banned by the Malaysian government. Small militant groups that engage in violence have even appeared in Malaysia. Fortunately, adherents of such groups are few in number.

Gender and religious revivalism

More orthodox or fundamentalist versions of Islamic revivalism believe that Muslim women should behave in certain ways, e.g., follow strict dress codes. In response, groups such as Sisters in Islam have risen to challenge such views. The important thing for non-Muslims to keep in mind is that different interpretations exist among Muslims, e.g., Saudi Arabian Muslim women are not allowed to drive cars while no such restriction has been imposed on Malaysian Muslim women. The Afghan "Taliban" version of Islam was especially strict in their policies towards women but they were even criticised by the conservative *mullahs* in neighbouring Iran and so on.

Malaysian cuisine

As mentioned earlier, the existence of many ethnic groups in Malaysia should be considered a culture-enriching plus rather than as a "problem". For example, Malaysian cuisine has been greatly enriched by the cuisine of the various ethnic groups. "Hainanese chicken rice" with its delicious sauce made up of pounded chillies and garlic can only be found in Malaysia and Singapore. It cannot be found on the island of Hainan in China! The other Chinese dialect groups also have their own culinary specialities, e.g., *yong tau foo* (Hakka), *char kway teow* (Hokkien), *bak kut teh* (Hokkien), etc. Similarly, Malay cuisine has been enriched by the cuisine of the Indian subcontinent and Thailand (*tom yam* soup). Malay cuisine includes the mouth-watering *satay* and *nasi lemak*. Indian cusine includes North Indian food (the so-called Mughal food) and South Indian food. There are also *halal* versions of Chinese and Indian cuisine available to Muslims in Malaysia. Food is an integral and wonderful part of Malaysian culture and this fact should be happily celebrated. It should also be used to enhance the experience of foreign tourists in Malaysia.

Ethnic and cultural diversity as a plus in Malaysia

The ethnic diversity of Sarawak and Sabah is also a wonderful thing that should be celebrated by all Malaysians. Indeed the Sarawak state government has capitalised on this to promote its Rain Forest Music Festival that features Sarawakian music groups in addition to invited musical groups from other countries.

We Malaysians should be proud that in this small nation of ours, we can find such a rich diversity of cultures. For example, the Chinese with their lion and dragon dances; the Malays with their *wayang kulit, kuda kepang*, etc.; the Indians with their classical Indian dances; and the East Malaysian natives with their music and other cultural riches.

Chapter 9

Children, Youth and Social Problems

As fertility drops in Malaysia over time (e.g., the number of children born per family declines), the number of young people as a percentage of the total population will also decrease. Although there will be fewer children and teenagers in relation to adults in the future, as Malaysians become more affluent because of industrialisation and further economic growth, parents will spend more on their children. Also, children and teenagers will have more purchasing power as their parents give them more money to spend and as more of them work part-time during the school holidays and so on. Thus, we can expect the market for products and services used by children and teenagers to grow over time, e.g., products for newborns and babies, childcare services, educational services for children, musical products and entertainment services for kids and adolescents, clothes for children and teenagers, etc. One potential problem is that our children and teenagers may become more materialistic and consumerist with this growing affluence. The need to conform, to purchase and own what their friends and peers already possess, to keep up with the latest fashion trends and to be part of the "in crowd", etc. will be strong. Thus, children and teens from low income families may feel deprived if they cannot buy and own the latest trendy clothes and consumer products. Some teenagers and youths may even resort to shoplifting in order to possess these goods (as in neighbouring Singapore) or even to prostitution in order to obtain the money to buy these goods (as in Japan).

Nevertheless, the vast majority of Malaysian children and teenagers grow up to be productive, law-abiding and tax-paying citizens. Even so, some do "go astray" and cause harm to themselves, their families or to the larger society. In order to channel the excess energy and idealism of teenagers and youths, it is necessary for the larger society to give them the opportunity to join clubs, societies and organisations that contribute to personal growth or to societal betterment. Otherwise, some may be drawn into religious cults or extremist religious or political organisations. Examples of organised bodies that are beneficial for children and teenagers include social-welfare organisations that provide help to the poor, elderly and chronically ill; sports and adventure clubs; societies that promote cultural activities; and clubs and societies that promote personal growth and learning such as the Scouts. The Malaysian government may also want to consider setting up volunteer groups similar to the American "Peace Corps" except that our version can have the option of doing voluntary service either within Malaysia itself or overseas. Our young volunteers can help to teach older Malaysian folks in the countryside who are illiterate to read and write. Others can help disadvantaged rural children and urban children from squatter families with their studies and also to serve as positive role models for them. For example, Puteri UMNO volunteers have begun going to the *kampungs* to help rural kids to improve their English. This is a good start and the programme should be expanded.

Teenage delinquency and crime

Some social scientists believe that there is a relationship between the numbers of teenagers and young adults in a population and the number of crimes committed. Since it is a fact that most crimes are committed by teenagers and young adults, therefore, if the percentage of teens and young adults in a population is high, then the number of crimes committed would also be high. However, we should remember that other factors may also affect the crime rate, e.g., whether the country is mostly rural and agricultural or mostly urban and industrial, whether the family as a social institution remains strong or whether single-parent families are found in large numbers, whether the unemployment and underemployment rates are high, whether the production and sale of illegal drugs has corrupted the society and so on. It is interesting to note that the Japanese crime rate is relatively low compared to that of the U.S. although both are highly urbanised and industrialised societies with low fertility. It also seems that teenagers in Malaysia tend to experience less angst as compared to their counterparts in the U.S., e.g., violent behaviour is less prevalent among Malaysian teenagers, drug and alcohol abuse rates are lower, etc.

The health of teenagers and young adults

The teenage years are a time of transition and development (physical, mental and social) and some teenagers may engage in high-risk behaviour or what is regarded by adults as delinquent behaviour. People often first begin smoking tobacco, drinking alcohol or taking narcotic drugs during their teenage years because of curiosity, peer pressure, rebellion or advertising that glamourises such behaviour. The problem of course is that things such as nicotine in tobacco, etc. are highly addictive and when the teenagers become adults, they may be "hooked" and find it very difficult to quit smoking. Teens who take harder drugs such as ecstasy, ketamine and heroin may end up with permanent damage to their health and ruin their future social and economic lives.

Teenagers and young adults are also at higher risk of attempting suicide or engaging in risky behaviour such as dangerous driving. Other teens may engage in loose and unprotected sex and risk contracting sexually-transmitted diseases, ending up with unplanned pregnancies and so on. The Malaysian authorities need to focus on preventing such problems among the teenaged and young adult subpopulations. Similarly, Malaysian parents need to realise that children and teens need parental attention and supervision and that such needs cannot be substituted with short amounts of so-called "quality time" or abundant material goods for the kids. There was a very interesting series on American Public Television (APT) called *The Lost Children of Rockdale County* which discussed the root causes of signs of troubled teens such as drug abuse, sexual promiscuity, suicides, delinquency, etc. among white middle-class kids in a relatively affluent suburb of Atlanta, Georgia. One expert commented that the problem is due to clueless, "lost parents" (who either neglect their kids or are overly permissive with them) rather than "lost children". If Malaysian parents are not careful with their children but spend so much time working that their children are neglected or inadequately supervised, social problems among Malaysian teenagers will definitely increase. The transcript for the APT series can be accessed at: *http://www.pbs.org/wgbh/pages/frontline/ shows/georgia/.*

The children and teenagers of today are the productive citizens of tomorrow. We need to nurture them carefully and invest in them to reap the benefits and avoid the costs of failing to do so tomorrow. Thus, we have to ensure that children will not grow up malnourished in poorer families, e.g., by having the government provide "child allowances" to families with children (as in certain progressive European nations), by providing subsidised school meals to students from poor families and so on.

Social science and educational research has shown that students from socioeconomically deprived families are less likely to do well in their studies compared to those from better-off families. In order to improve their academic performance and make sure that they get the education necessary to function effectively in the knowledge economy, weak students must be identified as early as possible in primary school so that action can be taken to help them to improve. If this is not done, weak students will fall further and further behind their peers and eventually, at the end of Standard Six or Form Three, they will leave school as semi-illiterates and have difficulty finding work. This is because as the Malaysian economy changes, more and more industrial and service-sector jobs will be created while agricultural and manual jobs will shrink in number. The MCA has launched the "Langkawi Project" to help weak students to improve in their studies. If projects like these are truly effective, they should be expanded to cover all students who need help with their studies.

On the other hand, good students from socioeconomically deprived families should not be neglected either. They should be identified and assisted financially through loans or direct grants so that they can maximise their education and achieve their full potential.

Chapter 10

Gender Issues
in Malaysia

THE term "sex", as used by social scientists, refers only to the biological and physical differences between men and women. When social scientists use the word "gender", we refer specifically to what a particular society defines to be the "proper" behaviour, roles, etc. expected of males and females respectively. In other words, gender is not the same as "sex". Gender is therefore said to be "socially constructed" (made by human beings and human society). For example, in Malaysian society, males are expected to behave in ways "appropriate" to their sex while females are also expected to behave in ways "appropriate" to their sex. People who do not act according to such social expectations (e.g., men who like to dress in women's clothes and women who smoke and drink heavily) will be subjected to strong negative reaction by the rest of society. Expectations of appropriate behaviour for women can

differ drastically in different societies. All we need to do is
to think of how Afghan women were expected to dress and
behave during the Taliban regime's rule in Afghanistan,
how the Saudi Arabian government continues to forbid
women from driving cars in that country, how women
behave in Western countries such as Sweden and the U.S.,
etc. to illustrate this point.

Unequal life chances for women as compared to men in Malaysia

Gender is an important issue because it is strongly linked to
socioeconomic inequality and unequal life chances for
women. "Life chances" refer to the chances of getting a
good education and the chances of achieving positions
high in power, prestige and wealth later on in life. In most
societies, women have poorer life chances than men as a
result of gender expectations and outright discrimination.
In politics, few women hold powerful positions such as that
of prime minister or president of a nation. Often, those
who end up in these positions do so because their fathers or
husbands were powerful politicians. Women tend to be
underrepresented in Parliaments and National Assemblies
in most nations. This is also the case in Communist
countries where there is supposed to be equality between
men and women. Women are also underrepresented in
Cabinets and the top ranks of the civil service, the police,
the armed forces and in private-sector companies. Women
who are Cabinet ministers are often given relatively
unimportant positions such as Minister of Social Welfare
while important positions such as Minister of Finance,
Home Affairs, Foreign Affairs, Defence, etc., tend to be

held by men. In Malaysian politics, the only woman who has managed to hold a powerful ministerial position in the Malaysian Cabinet is Rafidah Aziz. Feminists often complain of laws passed by male-dominated Parliaments which ignore the needs of women or which actually discriminate against women. For example, the foreign wife whose marriage to a Malaysian husband ends in divorce is subject to deportation from Malaysia no matter how long she has lived in this country and despite the fact that her children are Malaysian citizens.

Malaysian women, like women in other countries, are subjected to "vertical occupational segregation" and also to "horizontal occupational segregation". Vertical occupational segregation means that there are fewer and fewer women the higher up one goes in an organisation or a profession. For example, most chief executive officers and general managers of big companies are men while most clerks, secretaries, etc. are women. Women tend to be concentrated in so-called "women's jobs" such as nursing and clerical work which often do not pay well and do not have much prestige. This concentration of women in certain kinds of jobs is called horizontal occupational segregation. Women may also be discriminated against when it comes to job hiring and promotion. This is especially true for certain kinds of jobs dominated by men.

Other disadvantages faced by women: sexual harassment and domestic violence

Women may also experience sexual harassment from male supervisors and bosses while at work. "Sexual harassment" refers to unwelcome attention of a sexual nature. In some countries, there are no laws to protect women against sexual harassment. Fortunately, in Malaysia, there are laws that theoretically serve to protect women against sexual harassment.

Women are often disadvantaged socially also. In the family, sons may be treated better than daughters, e.g., sons are given more freedom, daughters have to do more of the housework in families without maids, parents may spend more on educating sons than daughters. Literacy rates and educational achievement of women tend to be lower than that of men. (However, this may be changing as more and more women enter higher education in Malaysia.) After the death of parents, sons may also inherit more property than daughters. One of the most extreme cases of social discrimination against females can be found in China and India today, i.e., the problem of "sex selective abortion" whereby an unborn baby girl is aborted simply because her parents prefer to have a male child instead of a female child. Hopefully, this is not occurring among Malaysian families.

Many women are subjected to domestic violence, e.g., they may be beaten up by abusive boyfriends or husbands. Domestic violence can result in mental distress, serious injuries and even death. In Malaysia, the Domestic Violence Act was passed in 1994 after many years of lobbying by women's groups.

Women often sacrifice their education or their careers for the sake of their husbands. They may stop schooling or drop out of the labour force after getting married and after giving birth. Working women often suffer from the "Double Burden of Women" or the "Supermom Syndrome". Although they work full-time outside the home, they are also expected to handle most of the household responsibilities and take care of the children when they get home. Divorce often hurts the wife more than the husband. This is especially true of housewives and of women who have sacrificed their education or careers for the sake of their husbands and children. Divorced women often suffer substantial downward social mobility, i.e., they can suffer steep drops in family income and standard of living after a divorce. If a divorced woman is granted custody of the children but the ex-husband does not contribute financially in terms of regular child-support payments, this would make her life even more difficult.

In the eyes of feminists, many religions also treat men and women unequally. This view is controversial in that those who are devout followers of a particular religion may deny this assertion vehemently. Still, no one can deny that in Roman Catholic Christianity, women are not allowed to be priests. In Islam, men are allowed to have four wives but women are not allowed to have multiple husbands. Also, it is much easier for a Muslim man to divorce his wife than for a Muslim woman to divorce her husband.

Some people argue that women usually earn less than men because women tend to have less investment in "human capital" (in the form of education, training and so on) than men. Also, they argue that women are more likely to experience career interruption than men, e.g., women may drop out of the labour force temporarily or permanently after they give birth. Some women who return to work after childbirth choose to work part-time. This will affect the chances of career success for the women.

Feminists recognise that there is often strong discrimination against women in many societies. They point out that the traditional sexual division of labour in industrial society works to the disadvantage of women—men participate in the "public sphere" which brings more reward in terms of power, prestige and wealth while women are in the "private sphere" (domestic sphere) where they do unpaid work (housework, child-rearing, etc.) and do not earn money and are socially isolated. Furthermore, the job market often works to the disadvantage of women, e.g., to be promoted, the employee often has to work late, work on weekends, go on business trips, accept transfers to other towns and so on. The family obligations of women often prevent them from doing all these. Working women often suffer from the "Double Burden of Women" or the "Supermom Syndrome", i.e., they not only work outside the home but they also have to handle household responsibilities and take care of the children after getting home from work.

Feminists argue that one way to reduce gender inequality is to change the socialisation of boys and girls. For example, Malaysian girls can be brought up to be more ambitious, to be more assertive and so on. Males can be brought up to regard women as fellow human beings worthy of respect, to treat women equally and so on. Feminists also argue that there should be stronger laws against gender discrimination when it comes to the hiring and promotion of employees.

Chapter 11

Social and Other
Changes in Malaysia

THE changes that have occurred in Malaysia over the last
few decades since Independence have been tremendous.
With the success of Malaysia's industrialisation policy
through the encouragement of foreign direct investment
and export-oriented production of industrial products, the
rate of social change has accelerated. Today, the structure
of the Malaysian economy has changed from that of an
agricultural nation heavily reliant on the export of primary
commodities such as rubber and tin to that of an industrial
and service economy. It has been claimed that Malaysia is
the 17th largest exporter in the world. Economic growth
and job availability in areas such as Penang Island, the
Klang Valley and southern Johor has spurred outmigration
from the rural areas and small towns. Thus, about 65 per
cent of Malaysia's population is urbanised today. The trend
of rural to urban migration can only intensify.

Rapid economic growth has also attracted foreign labour into the country (both legal as well as illegal). Thus, there are at least a million foreign workers from Bangladesh, Indonesia, the Philippines, etc. in Malaysia today.

Although foreign labour does help to spur economic growth by providing a pool of cheap labour, over the long run, it is preferable to reduce Malaysia's reliance on unskilled foreign labour (while stepping up efforts to recruit skilled foreign labour). If unskilled foreign labour is readily available, they would:

- Reduce pressures on local manufacturers to mechanise, upgrade technology and increase production efficiency
- Exert downward pressure on or even undercut the wage rates of unskilled and semi-skilled Malaysian workers
- This would in turn create tensions and social problems between low-skilled Malaysian workers and foreign workers

In 1983, the Malaysian government announced its policy of "privatisation", i.e., "... transfer to the private sector of activities and functions which have traditionally rested with the public sector". It involves any of the following components: management responsibility, assets or the right to use assets, and personnel. According to the government, privatisation of public services would lead to gains in efficiency, induce corporations to expand through greater utilisation of growth opportunities, relieve the administrative and financial burden of the Malaysian government, and also increase *Bumiputera* participation in the corporate sector. The government has also expressed the view that privatisation would allow the retention of experienced personnel through the payment of higher and more competitive wages.

The record of privatisation has been decidedly mixed: privatised companies such as Tenaga Nasional and Telekom Malaysia are providing acceptable levels of services (even if at higher prices) but other privatised entities such as Malaysia Airlines (MAS) lost a lot of money and were eventually "rescued" financially by the government. Some Malaysian intellectuals have criticised this phenomenon of "bailouts" of failing privatised corporations using public funds. Harsher critics have labelled the entire process of privatisation as "piratisation" (as in "pirates"), i.e., questionable transfer of valuable public assets to private hands. This phenomenon can also be called "privatisation of profits and socialisation of losses". Socialisation of losses includes "reverse privatisation" or "renationalisation" whereby the government takes over ownership and control of financially troubled privatised entities from their erstwhile private-sector owners.

Social and cultural changes

Industrialisation and the New Economic Policy have resulted in the appearance of a Malay middle class and a Malay working class and also accelerated the movement of Malays from the *kampungs* to the urban areas. The Malay community apparently is afflicted by relatively high rates of social problems as compared to other major groups such as the Chinese, e.g., a disproportionate number of drug addicts are Malays (although Malays comprise only about 65 per cent of the total Malaysian population, the percentage of drug addicts who are Malays is much higher). The famous French intellectual and sociologist Emile Durkheim argued that overly rapid social change can lead to a breakdown of traditional norms, values, community ties and other restraints on individual behaviour and thus result in self-destructive conduct (including suicide). It is possible that the high rates of social problems among Malays are due in some way to the rapid and disorientating changes in the Malay community over the last few decades, i.e., massive rural to urban migration; transformation from peasant to proletarian (industrial worker) in one generation; the clash of urban, commercial and capitalist values with the traditional values of the *kampung* and so on. The Islamic revivalism so obvious among the Malays during the last two decades is possibly another reaction to these rapid and disorientating social and economic changes.

A worrisome phenomenon that has emerged over the last few years is the appearance of an Indian urban "underclass" of poorly educated, unskilled and low-income people living in unhealthy, high-crime squatter areas of large cities such as Kuala Lumpur. Some of these people have been forced to migrate to the urban areas because they have lost their jobs and their homes as rubber and oil palm plantations have been bulldozed and replaced with industrial parks, shopping malls or housing estates. These victims of "development" have been geographically as well as socially displaced (often with grossly inadequate financial compensation in spite of years of loyal service to the owners of the rubber and oil palm plantations). Their children grow up in deprived circumstances and in urban squatter environments which put them at high risk of becoming delinquent or worse. The Malaysian government definitely needs to take drastic action in order to interrupt the emergence and consolidation of this Indian "underclass". Educational and job opportunities need to be expanded for Indian squatters and their children who have been displaced from the plantations.

Other groups that have benefited little from Malaysia's economic development include the *Orang Asli* in West Malaysia and some of the indigenous peoples of East Malaysia. The *Orang Asli* have been largely bypassed and remain overwhelmingly poor, lowly-educated and afflicted by high rates of malnutrition and disease. School dropout rates are so high that very few *Orang Asli* are university graduates. As for the situation of indigenous people in East Malaysia, some of the Sarawak natives have been fighting against displacement from their customary land by the activities of timber companies or by megadevelopment projects such as the Bakun Dam. Unfortunately, stereotypes of "backward" *Orang Asli* and other Malaysian indigenous groups persist in Malaysia.

Women's rights and feminist groups have emerged in Malaysia. Although largely middle class in composition, they are contributing to changing perceptions of "appropriate" roles for women in Malaysian society. Today, women engineers, doctors, lawyers, college lecturers, managers and other professionals are no longer a rarity even if high-level positions in these professions continue to be dominated by men. This is partly due to rapid expansion of the economy through industrialisation coupled with growth of the service sector. It also due to an increase in educational opportunity for young Malaysian females. Well-educated women are less likely to put up with the blatant sex discrimination that was so widespread in the past. Another possible reason for the appearance of feminist and women's rights groups in Malaysia could be the activism of female Malaysians who studied overseas in countries such as the U.S. and who were exposed to Western feminist ideas. Women's rights groups have also emerged among Malaysian Muslims who are females, e.g., the group called Sisters in Islam. This is in spite of the opposition of certain highly conservative, male-dominated "Islamist" groups who hold very rigid ideas of the "proper" place of Muslim women in particular and women in general in Malaysian society.

As Malaysian women become better and better educated (and it is interesting to note that Malay women appear to be doing better when it comes to higher education than Malay men) and participate in the labour force at higher rates, they are marrying later, having fewer children and also delaying childbearing. These latter developments have resulted in falling fertility rates (especially among the Chinese). Today, it is uncommon to find Malaysian Chinese families with "football team" size families of ten or more children. Even "basketball team" size families are becoming uncommon among the Chinese in Malaysia! (The powerful influence of social and economic forces on reproductive behaviour is clear if one keeps in mind the fact that traditional Chinese culture favoured large families with as many male children as possible.)

Falling fertility rates has resulted in "graying" and ageing of the population, i.e., the elderly as a percentage of the total Malaysian population is rising.

The Malaysian population has also become more mobile, i.e., migration from the rural areas to the urban areas is high and emigration to other countries (temporary or permanent) is also significant. High migration rates have resulted in families whose members are scattered all over Malaysia or even scattered all over the world. Thus, among Malaysian Chinese, it is not uncommon for a "transnational family" to have a son or daughter working in Singapore or Australia, another studying in Britain and the father spending part of his time travelling and working all over East and Southeast Asia.

As for cultural change in Malaysia, the most significant would be the continued influx of ideas from the West and the Islamic revival that first began stirring in the late 1960s and early 1970s. British colonialism has transformed what is now called "Malaysia" greatly. As a result of colonialism, Malaysian institutions such as its political system, a large part of its legal system, its economy during the first decade after Independence (with rubber and tin as the main exports), its education system, etc., show strong British influence. Other legacies of British rule include the heterogeneous composition of its population and the widespread use of the English language. Today, ideas continue to flow into Malaysian society from Britain and other English-speaking Western nations such as Canada, the U.S., Australia and New Zealand because large numbers of our people travel to these nations for higher education, the books and magazines we read are often imported from these nations and our foreign pop music and foreign television programmes and movies tend to be British and American products. For better or worse, young Malaysians often copy the behaviour of their Western counterparts (and recently their Japanese counterparts) too.

Islamic revivalism has also transformed the Malaysian social landscape. The most obvious is the change in dress among Muslim women and some Muslim men. Fewer Muslim women go outside the home with uncovered heads nowadays. Some Muslim men choose to dress in what they consider to be more "Islamic" style. Attendance at mosques and enrollment in religious schools (private as well as public) has increased. In the case of higher education, an International Islamic University (IIU) has been set up in Malaysia. "Islamic banking" has made its appearance also. Religious programming has increased in the mass media and *nasyid* music has even become bestselling music. Unfortunately, Islamic revivalism has also been accompanied by the appearance of extremist religious groups. Thankfully, these remain small and splintered and therefore, the religious (and ethnic) harmony of Malaysia is maintained.

Political change

Perhaps one of the most surprising developments in recent years is the political turmoil that emerged with the sacking, arrest, trial and imprisonment of the charismatic politician Anwar Ibrahim. These events were followed by unprecedented anti-government demonstrations in the Kuala Lumpur area. The demonstrations died down after a while but continued discontent with the government was indicated by the relatively strong showing of certain opposition parties in the general election of 1999. The then newly-formed political party Keadilan headed by Anwar Ibrahim's wife performed credibly while PAS did very well in the states of Kedah, Kelantan and Terengganu.

Another significant development is the appearance of non-governmental organisations (NGOs) dealing with issues such as consumer protection, the environment, women's rights, social justice, etc. These groups may be small and mostly middle class in composition but they have both enlivened and transformed Malaysian society as a whole. For example, the respected Consumers Association of Penang (CAP) publishes a relatively influential periodical called *Utusan Konsumer* as well as books and pamphlets. Environmental groups such as Sahabat Alam Malaysia (SAM) have increased environmental consciousness among certain segments of Malaysian society (ironically with "help" from the infamous haze blown in from Sumatra and Kalimantan in Indonesia beginning in the early 1990s). Women's rights groups such as Tenaganita and the Women's Development Collective have raised awareness of the problem of domestic violence in Malaysia. The social justice group called Aliran continues to point out the shortcomings of government policy and persistent inequalities in Malaysian society. The activities of all these NGOs are creating space for "civil society" in Malaysia.

The state of the Malaysian environment

Nevertheless, in spite of growing environmental consciousness (also called "Green consciousness"), the environment continues to deteriorate in Malaysia. Air pollution in big cities such as Kuala Lumpur is worsening largely because of the increasing number of motor vehicles on the roads and the increase in the number of factories accompanying industrialisation. Water pollution is also a problem: many of Malaysia's rivers are polluted with industrial and agricultural contaminants. A few years ago, the Klang Valley region even experienced water shortage and rationing. This situation arose because of increasing demand for water coupled with supply problems arising from deterioration of water catchment areas, polluted rivers, leakages and other wastage of processed water, etc. Besides air and water pollution, there is also solid waste pollution: the amount of rubbish and other solid waste being generated by our people is becoming larger and larger as Malaysia becomes more and more of a "throwaway society". It is ironic that while Western countries become more and more "Green" in their consciousness and public policies, fast developing nations like Malaysia do not emulate them but continue pursuing rapid economic growth with little attention to environmental deterioration. Thus, Malaysia continues to promote its car industry (protected by tariff barriers) while paying inadequate attention to resulting problems such as air pollution, worsening traffic jams and resulting long commuting times, higher energy consumption, loss of more and more of the countryside to roads and highways, deterioration of mass tranport systems such as bus systems, etc.

The building of more roads and highways to accommodate the larger and larger number of cars and other vehicles has also contributed to the "urban sprawl", i.e., the spreading out of cities into the surrounding countryside following transport arteries such as roads and railway lines. In our opinion, urban sprawl leads to "uglification" of the landscape. Already, the area extending from Ampang and Gombak in the northeastern suburbs of Kuala Lumpur to Port Klang in the southwest is threatening to become an endless "concrete jungle". If no action is taken to protect trees and other greenery, one would eventually be able to drive from Kuala Lumpur to Port Klang without knowing where one city or town begins and where the next city or town ends!

Chapter 12

Malaysia Under Dr Mahathir Mohamad's Leadership

IN late 2003, the conductor's baton was passed, so to speak, from Dr Mahathir Mohamad to Abdullah Ahmad Badawi very smoothly. Mahathir has held the post of Prime Minister of Malaysia longer than any of his predecessors. He came to office in 1980 and transferred power to Abdullah Ahmad in 2003, thus he was Prime Minister for 23 years. Mahathir has, therefore, had sufficient time to shape the Malaysian political system, the economy and the larger Malaysian society to a significant extent.

At this juncture, we would like to encourage the interested reader who does not want to have to slog through dense academic prose to take a look at two non-academic books that have been written by two of Malaysia's leading social scientists, i.e., *Beyond Mahathir: Malaysian Politics and Its Discontents*, by Khoo Boo Teik of

Universiti Sains Malaysia, and M *Way: Mahathir's Economic Legacy*, by Jomo K.S. of Universiti Malaya. In the two books, Khoo and Jomo evaluated Mahathir's political and economic legacies respectively in a masterly fashion.

In this chapter, a short evaluation of Dr Mahathir's impact on Malaysian society will be presented. In terms of the economy, under his leadership, there has been significant economic growth as measured by increases in conventional indicators such as the GNP per capita (Gross National Product per capita) between 1980 and 2003. There has been real growth in the sense that GNP per capita has increased even after adjusting for inflation. Malaysia's industrialisation based on foreign direct investment has created many jobs and thus, unemployment and underemployment are no longer as serious as they used to be during the first two decades of independence. Nonetheless, we should not be complacent since minority ethnic groups such as the Indians in Malaysia (especially those who have been displaced from rubber and oil palm plantations when the plantations are converted into housing estates) are experiencing trouble in the employment market and many are ending up with low paying, menial jobs. Inflation appears to be under control according to official government statistics but since price-controlled items are included in the "basket" of goods and services used to compute the Consumer Price Index (CPI), one can argue that the official data actually underestimates the inflation rate. The older reader can make a crude estimation of inflation in Malaysia by doing the following: calculating how many per cent his or her salary has increased between 1980 and 2003 and calculating how many per cent the prices of the following have increased between 1980 and 2003—the price of an average visit to the doctor (GP or General Practitioner), the total cost of sending a child to a government primary school for one year (the cost should include only necessities such as uniforms, books, school bags, meals at school, school fees, transportation, etc. and exclude things like tuition centre fees), the cost of a double-storey link house (you can compare for high-growth areas such as the Klang Valley and low-growth areas such as Kuantan or Ipoh), the cost of a motorcycle, the cost of a medium-sized car, the cost of a kilogramme of rice, the cost of a bowl of *laksa* bought from a hawker in a coffeeshop, the cost of a haircut by an Indian barber, etc.

Economic growth, however, has been accompanied by widespread environmental deterioration. Air quality is noticeably bad in heavily industrialised areas such as the Klang Valley. It is made worse by the periodic "haze" that blows in from Sumatra or Kalimantan. Many rivers in Malaysia are heavily polluted by biological, chemical or physical contaminants. One would be a fool to go for a swim in rivers such as Sungai Klang especially as it approaches the sea! Other rivers such as the Sungai Rejang in Sarawak are becoming heavily polluted with silt because of deforestation upstream as a result of uncontrolled logging activities. One can easily notice that something is wrong by the colour of the river, i.e., brownish-looking rivers mean that they are carrying a heavy load of silt. In certain parts of Malaysia, solid waste pollution is becoming a challenging problem, e.g., in the Klang Valley, garbage dump and landfill sites are rapidly filling up as we increasingly become a "throwaway society" (i.e., we use up and throw away things without paying sufficient attention to conservation and recycling).

Malaysia's active encouragement of foreign direct investment was first begun by Tun Abdul Razak. However, it was accelerated during the late 1980s by Dr Mahathir and thus, he can be credited with the transformation of Malaysia from an exporter of agricultural and primary commodities such as rubber, tin, timber and palm oil into a leading exporter of manufactured goods (albeit as a result of investment by multinational corporations).

Industrialisation is inevitably accompanied by pollution but one can say that air pollution has been exacerbated in Malaysia by Dr Mahathir's policy of encouraging the growth of a Malaysian car industry under heavy tariff protection coupled with inadequate development of efficient public transport systems within and between cities and towns.

In the political area, Malaysia has managed to avoid civil war (after the defeat of the Communist Emergency in 1960) and separatist conflict and has remained reasonably united and "stable" during Mahathir's premiership. Race and ethnic relations are reasonably good but there have been worrying incidents such as the Kampung Medan mayhem a few years ago. Malaysia is politically stable, however, political observers have noted that the demonstrations and street conflict that occurred after the downfall of Anwar Ibrahim are unprecedented in Malaysian political history. Unlike Western countries, the demonstrations were not allowed to proceed peacefully but were suppressed with some degree of brutality by the police. To be fair, however, it should be noted that Anwar and his supporters were allowed to make their anti-regime speeches at his official residence up until his arrest. (However, this could be due to uncertainty about how to deal with the former insider-turned-strong critic Anwar Ibrahim rather than due to tolerance on Mahathir's part.)

During the rule of Dr Mahathir, power was increasingly concentrated in the hands of the executive (i.e., in the Prime Minister himself). Political scientists have noted that in British-style parliamentary political systems, concentration of power in the hands of the executive (as contrasted with the legislature or the judiciary) is a noticeable trend even in Western liberal democracies such as Britain. However, there is no doubt that Mahathir was so successful in concentrating power that he became the most powerful Prime Minister we have ever had. His successful battle with the judiciary in the late 1980s has been well described by Khoo. He has also gained a degree of success in curbing the powers and privileges of the royal houses of Malaysia. After his narrowly-won, bruising battle with political opponents within UMNO in the late 1980s, he was able to dominate UMNO until the fallout with Anwar Ibrahim. His domination of UMNO was indicated by the interesting and curious phenomenon of the UMNO Supreme Council making declarations that there will be "no contest" for the top position in UMNO in order to preserve party unity!

The suicide attacks on the twin World Trade Center buildings in New York City happened during the rule of Mahathir in Malaysia. This terrible event and the misguided American policy responses to it (especially the harassment of Muslims in America and the invasion of Iraq by American and other allied troops) has worsened radical "Islamic" terrorism in various parts of the world. Southeast Asia, including Malaysia, has not been spared. Fortunately, terrorist incidents in Malaysia have been few in number and minor in severity. (Unfortunately, it has been revealed that some Malaysians have been heavily involved in the plotting of events such as the bombing of an international class hotel in Jakarta.) The Malaysian government and our highly effective Special Branch of the police must be given credit for keeping "Islamic" terrorism under control. The only negative development is that terrorists and would-be terrorists have been arrested and detained under the much criticised Internal Security Act (ISA) rather than under other less arbitrary laws.

"Civil society" in the shape of activist non-governmental organisations (NGOs) have emerged and grown in Malaysia during the last twenty years. However, this has also occurred in neighbouring Southeast and East Asian countries such as Thailand, Indonesia and Taiwan. In fact, Malaysia has one of the weakest NGO communities in the Asia-Pacific region. This is not surprising because of how the Mahathir Administration regarded the NGO community, i.e., with suspicion and a certain degree of impatient tolerance coupled with occasional crackdowns.

As for the social arena, income inequality in Malaysia has grown especially when immigrant groups from Indonesia and the Philippines are taken into account. Economist Simon Kuznets argued in the so-called "Kuznets Curve" that income inequality always increases during the early phases of economic growth. Later, further economic growth leads to a reduction in income inequality (partly because the state creates transfer payment mechanisms, uses fiscal policy to reduce poverty, etc.). Income inequality is easily evident when one looks at the wealthy areas of the Klang Valley and compare and contrast them with slum communities. Ironically, sometimes because of rapid urban growth and other related forms of "development", expensive mansions are built right next door to rundown shacks in the suburbs of Kuala Lumpur! As is always the case, the rundown shacks will eventually be torn down because of the value of the land underneath and their residents will be displaced even from these unattractive-looking and barely habitable abodes.

Race and ethnic relations in Malaysia are much better than in many other multiethnic Third World developing nations. For this, all Malaysians of goodwill ought to rejoice. During the Mahathir years, there were only isolated incidents of ethnic-based violence—the most serious being the disturbances in Kampung Medan and nearby areas a few years ago. However, as Khoo pointed out, sometime during the late 1980s, the ruling coalition's leaders did allow hotheads in the youth wing of UMNO to get away with the making of irresponsible speeches at political rallies held in Kuala Lumpur. This is highly regrettable but fortunately, the resulting situation of ethnic tension did not erupt into any violence.

Malaysian women have made much educational and occupational progress during the Mahathir years. Indeed, it appears that today, Malay women are overrepresented in the Malaysian public universities as compared to Malay men. However, whether this will also lead to overrepresentation of Malay women in professional and managerial jobs eventually is a moot point. There has also been a backlash against this progress made by Malay women in the form of anti-female extremism masquerading as Islamic revivalism. Mahathir promoted a modernist version of Islamic revivalism but other people tried (and are continuing to try) to push for theocratic, extremist and even exclusionist versions. What is even worse are periodic attempts by certain people from a particular political party to try to shove their values concerning "appropriate" female attire, female behaviour, etc. down the throats of all Malaysian women irrespective of whether they are Muslim or non-Muslim. The effort of these Taliban-like extremists ought to be strongly resisted by all fair-minded and progressive Malaysians who believe in a multiethnic and tolerant society.

During Mahathir's tenure, effort has been made to further integrate the Western and Eastern halves of the nation in spite of the physical barrier of the South China Sea. A symbolic but very smart gesture, in our opinion, is the holding of the National Day parade in East Malaysia even if this is done only once in a while. Newspapers in West Malaysia have made an effort to publish more news originating from Sabah and Sarawak. Unfortunately, one negative result of this push for integration is the "ethnicisation" of politics in Sabah and Sarawak following the West Malaysian pattern.

Malaysian culture has been considerably strengthened and enriched as Mahathir liberalised cultural policy and removed previous restrictions on the expression of minority group culture (especially the culture of the Malaysian Chinese). Thus, under him, restrictions previously placed on the performance of the lion dance (come to think of it, quite a ridiculous restriction in the first place!), restrictions on the broadcasting of Chinese costume drama on television, etc. were eased or removed. As a pragmatist, he has also loosened the national language policy and promoted the greater use of the English language in order that Malaysians can perform better and more competitively in the increasingly globalised economy. Unfortunately, under him, the Malaysian press continued to remain government-controlled and even sycophantic and this has hindered the emergence of a Malaysian citizenry that is well-informed, critical but socially responsible and participates actively in civil society and the body politic. However, one interesting fact is that Mahathir's promotion of information technology and the Multimedia Super Corridor (MSC) has also inadvertently allowed some Malaysians to get around government control of information and the news, to become better informed and has even resulted in the appearance of dissenting and highly critical mass media such as the electronic newspaper called *Malaysia Kini*.

This book on Malaysia consists of research findings from social science researchers together with personal observations of Malaysian society as well as thoughts on where Malaysia is likely to go. In the remainder of this book, there are a number of essays on the topics "Knowledge Economy", "Globalisation", and "Needed: New Skills for Professional Success in the Globalised 21st Century". These essays have been included because of the growing impact of globalisation on Malaysian society and the need to cultivate a "Knowledge Economy" and acquire new skills in order to successfully adapt to globalisation. We hope that you will enjoy the rest of this book!

PART II

Chapter 13

The Challenge
of Creating a
Knowledge Economy

MALAYSIA, together with the rest of Asia, is facing
unprecedented challenges, of which one of the biggest is
the creation of a so-called "Knowledge Economy".
So-called because economic success is increasingly based
on superior knowledge. It is just that mainstream economic
theory has tended to ignore the obvious until fairly
recently. A knowledge economy, as the name suggests, is
based on the accumulation and productive use of
knowledge. But what is "knowledge"? If the thermometer
shows that the current temperature is 18°C, it would be
data. The local radio announcer, knowing that the average
temperature of Kuala Lumpur is 26°C, goes on air and
informs his listeners that it is an unusually cold day. That is
information. Upon hearing that, a newly-arrived tourist
from Finland would happily conclude that it would be
comfortable to spend the day exploring the streets of Kuala

Lumpur wearing just a cotton shirt and pants. To the amusement of the Finnish tourist, he may see most of the locals shivering miserably unless they are clothed in thick sweaters. Both parties receive the same information but their reactions are totally different because they have different knowledge and perceptions. The Finn is used to a cooler climate and knows that he would feel comfortable with a particular type of clothing at a particular temperature. Knowledge is therefore a combination of one's past experience, current information, and ultimately, one's personal judgment.

Each day, thousands of transactions are carried out in the stock exchange. Every transaction is done at a fixed price. The price information is made available to every potential buyer and seller at the same time. Using this information, someone decides to sell and another person decides to buy. Their decisions are based on their knowledge. Based on the seller's analysis, experience, judgment and so on, the seller concludes that the price is high enough at that moment and so he instructs the broker to sell. At the same time, the buyer uses his or her knowledge and concludes that the price is low enough and thus decides to buy. Here is the importance of knowledge: the information (price) is not the real deciding factor. Normally, there will be buyers and sellers at a wide range of prices. Knowledge determines what we do with the information we have. The cynics among us may point out that perhaps some people have access to "inside information" and therefore do not depend on knowledge to make important decisions. But we believe that even these people would still need to make a judgment as to the reliability of the "inside information". To stretch the example further, after many years of profitable investment, a successful investor may decide to publish the secrets of his or her success in the buying and selling of shares in a book. The successful investor's knowledge is now publicly available information. However, do you really believe that all those who buy the book would be able to replicate the author's success?

The problem with primary commodities

In many ways, countries are very much like human beings—after all, countries are made up of and run by human beings. When both are "young", perhaps one can consider them to have plenty of raw energy. Young people can readily take up physically challenging work like construction, farming, or soldiering. Newly independent developing countries are usually agriculture-based food and primary commodity producers. Their economies are geared towards feeding the people and producing primary commodities to export in order to earn foreign exchange. This parallels the young farmer who feeds his family with the fruits of his labour and sells the surplus (and other agricultural products from the farm) in the market for money. But as his children and grandchildren grow up, they would need to find gainful employment to sustain themselves. They could also become farmers but in time, two problems inevitably arise. Firstly, they will run out of land sooner or later. And as they produce more and more agricultural commodities, the prices would tend to drop. In the past, the quantity supplied was limited because there was only one producer. Now, the quantity increases because there are more suppliers. Secondly, if prices decline in the long run, the farmers would have to produce more just to earn the same amount of money. Initially, the farmers would not notice the problem because the customers may buy all that they produce. But over the long term, the farmers' rising productivity would result in a fall in prices.

Learning the lessons of history

When Malaya gained independence from Britain in 1957, it was the top producer of rubber and tin in the world. And for a time, these primary commodities were good enough for the economic health of the country. The people's standard of living increased steadily over time. Malaysia became a model for the developing world. In time, other developing countries learned how to do the same thing. At heart, growing rubber trees is not really that difficult—any tropical country with suitable soil and a relatively reliable labour force can do so. It was the organisation and management of plantations that was the key and Malaysia did not have a monopoly of this knowledge. In fact, the rubber tree itself is not native to Malaysia. It was the British who first smuggled rubber seeds out of Brazil and started the first rubber plantations in Malaya. Anyhow, rubber is still rubber whether it comes from Malaysia or Thailand or Indonesia.

That is the greatest disadvantage of being a commodity producer—commodity prices tend to fall in the long run as more and more suppliers enter the market and competition increases. Commodities are particularly sensitive to changes in supply and demand because there is no difference in a commodity produced by different sources. Buyers can switch easily from one seller to another—and price becomes the main differentiator. In the long run, prices have a floor only because producers will switch to the production of other commodities which are more profitable if the price of the first commodity becomes too low. Hence, many rubber plantation companies ultimately decided to cut down their trees and sell their land to housing developers when profits became too low. Some even became producers of houses themselves!

The producers of exhaustible commodities like oil are slightly luckier because they are relatively few in number and they could get together to form a cartel to limit supply and keep prices higher than normal. What many people do not realise is that even producers of essential commodities such as oil have to perform a fine balancing act since they can control prices only to a limited extent and only in the short term. Imagine if the price of oil keeps going up year after year without stopping. Eventually, when prices are high enough, several things will occur to bring prices down. At high prices, the buyers of oil will attempt to conserve the use of oil or look for other sources of energy. They will also buy less and less oil because they cannot afford the high prices. Some may go into recession and thus the demand for oil may fall drastically. In turn, the income of the oil producers will begin to fall too as they sell less and less. The irony is that the higher the price, the less the producers may earn in the long run! This was what happened after the OPEC countries tried to limit supply in the 1970s. The Western economies went into recession from the oil shocks of the 1970s and this ended up hurting the oil producers even more. The oil-producing countries had planned ambitious development projects that had to be funded and falling oil prices actually forced these oil producers to borrow money when their incomes fell! Thus, the sword of high commodity prices can cut both ways.

Over time, exploration intensified, new producers entered the market and increased supply. Certain oil-consuming countries even found new domestic sources of supply, e.g., the countries adjoining the North Sea in Europe. At the same time, the consuming countries began serious conservation efforts and consumed less oil. As supply increased, the price of oil fell to new lows for much of the 1990s. Ironically, the price of oil would not have stayed up for long even if new sources have not been found. At high price levels, oil consumers could conceivably develop and switch to alternative forms of energy such as nuclear, solar and wind power. Thus, oil producers can raise prices only to a limited extent before they begin to hurt themselves. Hence, like any other commodity producers, oil producers have only a limited control over the price of their commodity.

Commodities do not rule

The principle here is that primary commodity producers earn normal (read slim) profits in the long term because primary commodities can be produced relatively easily—under the right conditions and with the right knowledge. Therefore, true economic power lies not in the hands of those who physically possess the raw materials but rather with those who possess the knowledge to find/create, organise and manage the production of these commodities. Therein lies the rationale for the creation of a knowledge economy where the focus is not on the production of commodities and goods alone but more importantly, in the production of such knowledge.

Malaysia's response

While the term "knowledge economy" is relatively new, the Malaysian government has been aware of the power of knowledge for a long time. Much of the current economic success of the nation can be attributed to the shrewd creation or borrowing and use of knowledge to continuously reinvent ourselves so as to remain competitive. On the one hand, Malaysia has established world-class research institutions such as the Rubber Research Institute which extended our longevity as a competitive player in the rubber market, e.g., by coming up with higher-yielding trees. We parlayed our agricultural knowledge by replicating our success with rubber into the planting of oil palm. At the same time, Malaysian companies began to invest in plantations in lower-cost countries such as Indonesia. We have moved up to become the managers and organisers instead of mere producers. We have created a knowledge economy—in agriculture at least.

The new commodity

On the other hand, Malaysia has tried to gain new technology (and hopefully knowledge) by welcoming foreign investment with open arms. Through the years, this strategy has broadened the Malaysian economy by promoting the growth of the industrial sector through the introduction of new industries such as cars and electronics.

Malaysia has always tried to attract cutting-edge technology. Malaysia was one of the first countries outside the developed world to manufacture semiconductors. At its height, electronics made up 60 per cent of Malaysia's exports and we were the top exporter of computer chips in the world. The problem with high technology is that it has a very short life-cycle. What is cutting-edge this year can easily become obsolete next year. A rule of thumb for microchips is that we get double the computing capacity for only two-thirds of the original price every 18 months!

Even traditional primary commodity prices have never fallen this fast. While we pat ourselves on our collective back and think that we are catching up with the developed countries because we are now capable of making high-technology goods such as microchips, few of us realise that microchips are just as much a commodity today as rubber and palm oil. A microchip made in Taiwan or South Korea functions no differently from one made in Malaysia. And since the raw material—silicon—is available everywhere, the strongest barrier to entering the industry is the huge start-up cost. Today, Singapore is even more dependent on electronic exports than Malaysia. South Korea has become the biggest exporter of memory chips in the world. In some ways, dependency on technological commodities is even worse than dependency on traditional commodities. The price of microchips always trends lower while the product life-cycle also becomes shorter. A fabrication plant's technology costing billions of ringgit becomes obsolete within three or four years. For the sake of comparison, it takes mere months to build a new fabrication plant in a low-cost country but years to start up a new plantation. The boom-bust cycle inherent to traditional commodities is even more pronounced in the modern commodities such as computer chips. When the Internet boom ended, Singapore experienced its worst recession since independence in 1965.

The transitory state of industrialisation

Industrialisation has brought us great economic progress, more wealth and social peace. With its greater productivity and higher profits, industry is able to provide much better wages than agriculture. As a result, our standard of living has increased tremendously in a relatively short time. We have come to expect a certain level of creature comforts. We expect our wages to go up every year and we expect a bonus to boot. Yet this achievement can be more transitory than we think. By and large, we have grown fat on the production, not the design of the goods we make. More than 20 years after we first began to industrialise, we are still dependent on foreign technology transfer in order to make these goods. In essence, we are still the offshore production base of multinational corporations. As mentioned earlier, while we pat ourselves on our collective back and believe that we are "catching up" with the developed countries because we are now capable of making high-technology goods such as microchips, few of us realise that microchips are just as much a commodity today as rubber and palm oil.

We can stay competitive as a producer of commodities—traditional or otherwise—as long as we can keep the cost of production low. One of the reasons why foreign investors were first attracted to set up factories in

Malaysia was our relatively low production costs. However, it is not easy to keep producing cheaply because as a country industrialises and experiences rapid economic growth, the cost of factors of production such as labour will rise. Even the country's currency may appreciate gradually as the country's assets increase. Over time, Malaysia has graduated out of the ranks of low-cost producers. To some extent, higher production costs was countered by rising productivity. A rising standard of living is usually accompanied by better educational facilities and better transport infrastructure. Therefore, even as a foreign investor has to pay more to hire a local worker, the average worker can now perform more sophisticated tasks because he is better educated. The better-educated worker can do the job of a few less highly-trained workers and therefore is better value to the employer even with higher pay. A better transport infrastructure also means that goods and raw materials can be shipped more efficiently and cheaply. However, in the production of commodities, rising productivity can offset rising costs only up to a limit. Since the production of commodities does not usually require much skill, new lower-cost competitors can easily come into the picture and make life more difficult.

Even as countries such as Malaysia transform themselves into newly industrialising countries (NICs), other Third World countries will also attempt to do the same. In time, Malaysia will be forced to make a hard choice—either to forego increasing wages and therefore freezing its standard of living or move upstream, i.e., turn towards the production of things that the new kids on the block do not have the skills to produce yet. Clearly, the first option is unattractive. Thus, in reality, Malaysia has been pursuing the second option for some time. The evolution from production of rubber to tyres and then to cars and microchips represents the unending movement to higher value-added and therefore more profitable commodities even as less technologically-advanced countries steadily take over the production of the lower value-added commodities. Yet no matter what commodity we move into—as long as it is a commodity—it is simply a matter of time before the competitors begin to catch up with us. Lest we think that this is a challenge unique to Malaysia, it has also happened to other nations before. We can therefore learn from their experiences.

What to keep and what to let go

Walk into any American supermarket and one will notice that "American" branded garments such as "Fruit of the Loom" are produced almost anywhere but in the U.S. Practically every piece of clothing is labelled "Made in China" (or Mexico or Pakistan). Open up any computer and one is almost sure to find chips labelled "Made in Malaysia" (or Korea) and disk drives "Made in Singapore" (or the Philippines). American (and European) manufacturers have increasingly moved the production of their goods overseas to countries with lower production costs. Even some high-tech hardware companies such as Xilinx only design chips: they outsource the actual production of their computer chips to other companies. This "hollowing out" of the manufacturing base has caused great bitterness among some sections of the American population—especially among workers who have lost their jobs as the actual manufacturing of these goods moved overseas. Lest we think that this is a purely Western phenomenon, Japan and even newly industrialising countries like Hong Kong and Singapore are already undergoing the same hollowing out of their industrial sectors to some extent. Hong Kong has moved the bulk of its manufacturing to China while Japan has been spreading its manufacturing facilities throughout Southeast Asia. Therefore, this hollowing out is not a Western phenomenon per se although it first started in the West. It began in the West because they industrialised much earlier and their living standards and production costs went up earlier too. These economic pressures forced their manufacturers to move to then-poorer countries such as Singapore and Hong Kong. In time, the same process worked its way through the Singapore, Hong Kong and Japanese economies and thus their manufacturers moved to Southeast Asian countries like Malaysia. Today, our turn is threatening to come.

Post-industrial countries produce knowledge

What do countries do when they have to move away from the production of commodities? The developed countries that have done so in the past refocused on the production and selling of knowledge and knowledge-intensive goods and services. They did not give up producing commodities totally but switched emphasis to the creation and discovery of new knowledge. Even with commodities which they had to give up producing, they retained and developed the know-how to create, manage and organise the production and marketing of these goods. The clothes and microchips may be made in other countries but these commodities are still designed in the advanced countries. The financial and strategic management of the manufacturers is still conducted from the originating countries. At the same time, these advanced countries carry out rigorous research—pure and applied—in every field. Research results in new knowledge. Much of the new knowledge that emerges does not result in immediate change. However, much of the new knowledge becomes building blocks for further research. From time to time, a discovery or invention results in products that are commercially exploited. Some of the new knowledge may even spawn entirely new industries. For example, the U.S. space programme created a need for new materials and led to the invention of Teflon which coats all our frying pans today. The laser which was used initially for targeting weapons is most commonly used today for entertainment (in CD and DVD players). The invention of the internal combustion engine gave birth to at least two industries—the car industry and the air travel industry which revolutionised travel all over the world. The invention of synthetic fibres such as polyester, nylon and rayon not only helped to rejuvenate the textile industry but they also helped the armour industry to produce things like helmets and bullet-proof vests.

Knowledge is more than mere information

Malaysians surely want our economy to be a knowledge economy. There is really no choice; ultimately, knowledge is the only resource that never runs out. In Malaysia, people often confuse information with knowledge. Therefore when people talk about the "knowledge economy", they are merely thinking of an economy driven by information technology or the so-called wired society. Many people think that by building a computer network and by having a computer connected to the Internet, they are now part of the knowledge economy. Not so fast! They have gained access to the greatest store of information on earth but information alone is not knowledge. Knowledge is what people do with information. South Korea and even Singapore are far more "wired" than the U.S. Yet few people would consider either to be a stronger knowledge economy than the U.S. If we look back at the stock investor example mentioned earlier (where everyone has the same information but only some of the people use the information profitably), it is easy to see that information is very different from knowledge. Information is public, knowledge is personal—imagine trying to get into someone's head and getting to know what he is thinking! Information is objective, knowledge is subjective or in the case of a country—cultural. Because knowledge is so personal or cultural, people or countries with the "right" knowledge can derive extraordinary profits from it.

What does it take?

What does it take to produce the "right" knowledge for a competitive economy? It takes exactly the same thing an investor needs to pick a winning stock every time. The right knowledge is a combination of many things. It is nearly impossible to know beforehand what that combination should be. Take the example of the scientist in charge of researching adhesives. He formulated a glue so weak that things stuck together by it can be blown apart by a strong breeze. For a glue, that would rate as a total failure. However, one day, a colleague of this person experienced some trouble while singing in church. He kept losing his page in his hymnal because the bookmark kept falling out. He needed something that would stick to the correct page but could also be peeled off easily so that it would not damage the page. That weak glue applied to strips of paper thus became the famous Post-it Notes. Today, that accidentally-discovered glue brings in millions of dollars in profits for 3M Corporation each year.

Since there is no way to tell what combination of knowledge will work best, the solution is to create as much knowledge and in as many areas as possible and then let them combine in a free-flowing fashion. So is there nothing a country like Malaysia can do to facilitate the creation of the knowledge it needs? There certainly is. It is a fairly safe assumption that some countries are better at creating knowledge than others. So what made them better? Knowledge is personal and subjective, i.e., it exists only within people. When we talk of a knowledge economy, we are really talking about the people within that economy. When we say a country is good at creating knowledge, what we are really saying is that the people from that country—as a group or culture—are good at creating knowledge. Every civilisation has its own golden age where its achievements outshone those of its peers at that time. If every culture is capable of excelling at creating knowledge, then what are the "drivers" for doing so?

The open society

People create knowledge from information. While information is not knowledge, it is a building block or prerequisite of knowledge. When we were children, our parents told us that fire is hot and we should not stick our hands into it. Some of us paid attention to this information and kept ourselves out of harm's way. But people can also create knowledge from experience. Even with the information given by our parents, some of us did confirm the hard way that fire *is* hot. Luckily, because of our reflexes, most of us escaped with the knowledge and maybe just a tiny scar. Because knowledge is built upon information and experience, people with more access to information and experience will naturally have more opportunity to create knowledge. Again, it is easy to think of information technology providing access to information but the world did not have the Internet until the 1990s. Long before the creation of the Internet, the knowledge economies of the world had already found effective ways of disseminating information to their people. In the U.S., there are libraries at the school, district (county) and city levels and this does not include the libraries supported by private endowments. For instance, Dallas, Texas—a city of some five million people—can tune into approximately 60 radio stations and literally well over a hundred television channels by cable or satellite—none of which are owned or even influenced by the government. While the quantity is impressive, what is even more crucial is the attitude of the people towards information.

People in Dallas discuss every topic under the sun with gusto. After all, 60 radio stations cannot be talking about the same topic from the same point of view all the time. People are free to choose what they want to listen to or talk about and therefore the society as a whole has an enormous breadth of knowledge. Rather than a lack of information, there is actually an overload of information. Depending on one's point of view, not all the knowledge is necessarily good or helpful. Let us think back to the example earlier of how a seller sells shares to a buyer at a single price, both driven by their individual knowledge. Only one of them can be "right" in terms of profit-making at any one time. So, half the people buying and selling shares are "wrong"! Still, as the saying goes, one cannot fool all the people all of the time and the diversity of viewpoints ensures that no single point of view will cause too much damage. Somehow in the midst of this Tower of Babel, the majority of people are able to come to balanced and well-considered opinions, by and large without violence. The few who don't are generally ignored by mainstream society until they come round to the majority's point of view or until the majority comes round to their point of view. The only time the U.S. as a country had not been able to "agree to disagree" peacefully resulted in the American Civil War of 1861-1865. There is nothing like the horrors of fratricide to drive home the value of tolerance of alternative viewpoints.

By comparison, the flow of information is less smooth in all Asian countries including Malaysia. There are far less channels for information dissemination. For example, there are only a limited number of television channels in Malaysia and most of these are owned by the government. The rationale for, if not the actual practice of censorship, is so ingrained that government ministers have been known to tell the press to practice less self-censorship. Most of the local news is either sensational or trivial or factual rather than analytical or argumentative. In Asian societies, many topics remain taboo and even illegal and most people want to sound and appear reasonable if not downright conformist. This lack of debate does not equal agreement but it is deemed necessary by the authorities for social peace.

In knowledge economies like the U.S., tolerance extends to experience as well. Within the boundaries of the law, everyone is free to do whatever he likes. However, we should not equate tolerance with acceptance. Just because one is free to do what one likes, it does not mean one will be more popular for it. Still, the country is so big and the society so diverse that one can always find a subculture to be happy in no matter what one's tastes may be. This tolerance creates a sense of security and freedom to experiment. Should one's experimentation prove mistaken and fails, one can always abandon whatever unusual lifestyle one is involved in and rejoin the mainstream. Part of this tolerance is a more forgiving attitude towards genuine mistakes. For example, individuals who go bankrupt suffer the same penalties as do bankrupts in Malaysia such as losing their possessions. However, the penalties only last for seven years and in many places, a person's home is protected from bankruptcy proceedings. In fact, the U.S. is in the process of becoming less forgiving at least where bankruptcy is concerned because people have been taking advantage of the process. But such "undesirable" events are stigmatised less heavily than in Asian societies.

There is no advocacy here that Malaysia should replicate the culture of Western societies such as the U.S. It should not and cannot because one can never really replicate another culture. Culture is a symbiotic thing—the members of a culture grow up in it and it in turn grows out of their collective beliefs, values and practices. Therefore it is impossible for Malaysia or any other countries—even another Western one—to fully replicate America's culture with respect to tolerance, inventiveness and technological progress. But it is to our benefit to analyse the sources of America's strength (and the West's strength) and to learn from them. While some people may choose to make anti-Westernism into a fashion statement, as a nation and as individuals, we do ourselves a permanent disservice if we object to learning from the West's strengths.

The openness and tolerance of their people is the key to making their societies so innovative. It is this willingness to debate original ideas and experience untried things that forms such a conducive environment for knowledge creation. The knowledge economy is not an invention of the West. As we have seen earlier, Malaysia has developed valuable knowledge too as has every other nation. But no nation can match the speed with which the U.S. innovates. Neither Japan with its manufacturing prowess, or Britain have the innovative capabilities of the U.S. In fact, Japan (which Malaysia looks to as a model), has stagnated in the last decade. Britain, after losing its empire, has settled into its role as just another European nation albeit one with a very colourful history. The emergence of the knowledge economy in the U.S. must have had its roots in some qualities of the society itself. The challenge Malaysia faces in turning itself into a knowledge economy is how willing are we to create an environment conducive to knowledge creation.

Do we really want a knowledge economy?

The challenge is not an economic but a cultural one and the price is high. The government does not create knowledge. The people create knowledge. The government can only hope to provide the conditions and environment necessary for the people's creativity to bloom. In the final analysis, the government is a creation of the people, by the people. Ironically, people often rail against the government but people do get the government they deserve. We can't have a knowledge economy without a knowledge society. Are the people sufficiently open-minded to evolve an open society? Are the people tolerant enough to allow innovation and non-conformity to flourish? Are the people mature enough to try not to stifle those whom they disagree with? Are they willing to change if those whom they disagree with are proven to be more correct? Innovation by definition *is* change. Are we willing to reward those who are talented and capable without any restrictions? If we don't, we will lose that talent. Talent and ability are in short supply the world over and if we don't give them the recognition they deserve, other countries are more than happy to welcome them. Our loss is their gain. The answers to these questions are unknown and may never be known.

Chapter 14

Globalisation: The Malaysian Experience and Challenges

IN 1910, a Scotsman and an Englishman through diverse circumstances found themselves thousands of miles away from home but the owners of some 500 acres of rubber estates in colonial Malaya. Opportunities were somewhat limited in their native island and they believed that their talent would be better rewarded in places where such talent was in shorter supply. They decided to pool their resources and properties together in the form of a limited company. Despite two world wars, several changes in governments, ups and downs in the prices of commodities, the company prospered. It acquired more land and slowly people came to respect its name. In time, it branched out into other businesses like tyres and heavy machinery. Making tyres was a natural choice because the company was already producing the main raw material for it. The company needed bulldozers to clear jungle land for planting. Since it had to buy and maintain a large fleet of bulldozers for itself, it might as well make a business out of it and hence the move into heavy equipment. In time, the profits from the heavy equipment division would exceed the profits from the plantation division.

As the company grew, so did its adopted country. Slowly, towns and cities grew nearer and nearer to some of the company's plantations. The land under the company's rubber trees was soon worth more than the latex coming out of those same trees. So the land was cleared again and this time, the company "planted" houses, malls, schools and roads instead of rubber trees. The company had moved into yet another line of business—property development. At the same time, the company also began to acquire land in other countries where land is still cheap enough to plant rubber and oil palm. The company is using the knowledge it has gained at home to create similar product life cycles in other less-developed countries. Today, this company is one of Malaysia's handful of multinational corporations, operating in 19 countries including Hong Kong, Australia, United Kingdom and New Zealand, with over 26,000 workers. Its assets are equivalent to 5 per cent of Malaysia's GNP. Its profits exceed a billion ringgit in 2001. As a sign of how globalised the company has become, 58 per cent of this billion ringgit came from the company's businesses overseas. By contrast, plantations—local or otherwise—contribute less than 8 per cent of total profits today. Surely, the company's founders, William Middleton Sime and Henry Darby, would be extremely proud of the company they founded if they could see it today.

In 1971, oil was discovered off the Terengganu coast. Petronas, the national oil company, was formed three years later and the first shipment of crude oil followed a year later. At that time, Malaysia had little experience in offshore exploration and production of petroleum. Malaysia depended on multinational oil corporations like Esso and Shell for expertise and technology to find and drill for oil. Displaying enormous foresight, Petronas quickly learned to acquire the expertise and technology and within ten years, successfully struck oil on its own in the Dulang oilfield. Capitalising on its knowledge and experience, from 1990 onwards, it quietly but quickly expanded into a global player, repeating its homegrown success in Vietnam, China, Iran and Sudan. As a measure of Petronas's success, Sudan became a net exporter of oil for the first time in 1999.

Much like Sime Darby, Petronas was not contented to stick to exploration and production only but quickly expanded downstream using the home market as a testing ground to hone its skills. Petronas opened the first Petronas petrol station in 1981. Petronas Dagangan Bhd. was formed in 1982, listed on the Kuala Lumpur Stock Exchange (KLSE) in 1994, and by 2002 it was the second biggest distributor of petroleum products in Malaysia with 33 per cent of the market. The knowledge and experience gained from this venture allowed Petronas to bid for and gain control of Engen—South Africa's biggest oil refiner and petrol retail network—in 1998. Engen controls nearly one-third of the petrol retail market in South Africa and today contributes 20 per cent of Petronas's annual earnings. Petronas has become a truly globalised corporation operating in 32 countries. Profits from overseas operations, including exports, make up 75 per cent of the corporation's revenues.

Themes of globalisation

Both corporations are examples of how healthy, well-managed companies eventually grow beyond the bounds of home and become global entities. As a nation that had prospered under free trade, we regard such companies as models of success. The growth and success of corporations like these have some common themes that have broad implications for Malaysia Incorporated. Firstly, global corporations like these often had foreign links. Many, especially the older companies, were started by foreigners and may well be subsidiaries of foreign corporations still. Foreign ownership and support is normal when we are still undeveloped or the business involved technology we have not yet mastered. For such new businesses, there will be a large inflow of foreign capital, skills, and equipment. Indeed, we might not have been able to succeed in or even enter such businesses were it not for the help of foreigners who already had the expertise at that time. For example, Malaysia may not have developed a rubber industry if the British had not brought the rubber plant to the country and started the first rubber estates. Petronas would probably not have been able to grow so fast if it had not been able to draw on the expertise and technology of its partners, Esso and Shell, from day one. Today, Esso is still 65 per cent owned by Exxon Mobil Corporation of the U.S., the largest oil company in the world, just as Shell is 75 per cent owned by Shell Overseas Holdings Ltd. of Britain.

Secondly, after these companies have established themselves at home, they used their knowledge and experience and replicated themselves overseas. If a rubber plantation uses its land to build houses, then it has less land to plant rubber. It could buy more land further away from urban areas and create new plantations but as the whole country develops, land and labour prices rise and ultimately, the rubber company either moves its rubber planting activity to a less-developed country or gives up planting rubber altogether. For an oil company, expansion overseas is imperative for survival. There is a finite amount of oil under each country. At the current rate of production, Malaysia will have no more oil to export in less than 10 years. New discoveries will occur but that is merely delaying the inevitable. If Petronas is to survive, it has no choice but to globalise. Given Petronas's average net profits of more than RM5.5 billion ringgit a year, its well-being is a matter of national concern indeed.

People

Perhaps one can say that globalisation is as natural a process to companies as breathing is to people. Although the label "globalisation" is new, the process itself is not. Globalisation refers to the process of welding together of the economies of different countries through the free flow of trade, capital, people and knowledge and technology. As we have seen from the examples above, Malaysia is no stranger to globalisation. There would have been few Chinese and Indians in Malaysia today if their ancestors had not been needed in the tin and rubber industries at the beginning of the nation's development. Today this human flow continues with Indonesians and Filipinos being the latest arrivals in Malaysia. By 1997, one out of every four workers in Malaysia was foreign. The plantation industry depends on foreign workers for over 60 per cent of their work force, while the figure for the construction industry is 70 per cent. Large numbers are entering the manufacturing industry as well. This large inflow of foreign labour is essential to keeping Malaysia's wage costs low—real wages grew about 3 per cent for the whole of the 1990s. Without this inflow of cheap labour, Malaysia's competitiveness in manufacturing would have been eroded long ago.

Knowledge and technology

The rapid development of Malaysia, to a large extent, has been due to both our trading partners' willingness to transfer technology to us and our ability to absorb it. Foreign investors come not only with the capital and manufacturing equipment to set up new businesses and industries. They also bring knowledge of production methods, management techniques and access to overseas markets which can be even more valuable than capital. This was dramatically demonstrated by the electronics industry in Malaysia. It took just 20 years from the setting up of the first semiconductor plant in Malaysia by Motorola to the phenomenon of Malaysian-designed and produced microchips (albeit, based on technology bought from Japan). Malaysia has also been unstinting in its investment in education. In the Sixth Malaysia Plan (1991-1995), 15 per cent of the development expenditure was earmarked for education. By the 1990s, 99 per cent of Malaysian students were completing primary school—thus we have practically achieved universal literacy in a generation. Yet the quality of education is not as high as it could or should be. The racial quotas put in place to create an educated *Bumiputera* middle class also unintentionally gave merit a lower priority at the university entry level. Simultaneously, the use of Malay as the medium of instruction led to lower proficiency in the English language (most critically at the tertiary level). This language gap is contributing to a dip in educational standards as most advanced research is published in English. However, the government has been very adaptive in attempting to redress the deficiency by increasing the use of English in local universities, allowing private educational institutions to use English, and allowing foreign universities to establish branch campuses in Malaysia.

Foreign investment and trade

The IMF reported that developing countries' share of world trade has increased from 19 per cent to 29 per cent from 1971 to 1999. Malaysia benefited greatly from this boom of foreign investment and trade and was transformed during that time period. In 1970, Malaysia was essentially a producer of tin, rubber, palm oil, and timber—these primary products made up 78 per cent of Malaysia's exports while manufactured goods made up 12 per cent of which just 1 per cent was electronics and electrical products. Total exports then amounted to only US$1.6 billion.

By 2000, primary products had declined to make up only 12 per cent of Malaysia's exports. Manufactured goods increased to make up 85 per cent of our exports of which 62 per cent are electronics and electrical products. Total exports have grown to over US$98.2 billion. In that time period, real GNP per person grew from about US$800 to US$2,400 even though the population also grew from 13 million to about 20 million. To put that achievement in more comprehensible terms, in 1970, 49.3 per cent of the people in West Malaysia lived in poverty. By 1990, the number had dropped to 6 per cent according to official statistics. This rapid industrialisation made Malaysia one of the top ten fastest growing economies in the world. These achievements would not have been possible without the employment and income generated by rapid expansion in export-oriented manufacturing.

Capital

The phenomenal growth that transformed Malaysia from the mid-1980s onward and ensured the success of the NEP was powered in greater part by foreign direct investment. Seventy-five per cent of our manufactured exports were produced by foreign multinational corporations which also employed 45 per cent of the work force. This is in line with the experience of young nations all over the world where the flow of capital in the form of foreign direct investment or foreign aid has been instrumental for the uplifting of their developing and underdeveloped economies. Such economies by definition have relatively little capital and therefore have very limited resources for business formation, job creation and other economic activities that set these economies on the upward spiral of wealth creation. An injection of capital (together with the knowledge and trade) could kickstart these economies as indeed happened to the devastated economies of East Asia and Western Europe after World War II. By and large, it worked well for Asia for 50 years. For most of this period, capital was scarce and whatever capital that flowed into Asia was put to good use. Within 40 years after World War II, both areas had become some of the world's richest economies.

However, beginning in July 1997, the inflow of capital unexpectedly became a massive outflow resulting in major economic upheavals across Asia, including Malaysia. The outflow was triggered by speculation against the currencies of several Asian countries and which depressed their values significantly. Panicked foreign investors, fearing the devaluation of their investments, withdrew their capital hastily, thus turning the attack on the currencies into a crisis. Inappropriate remedies mandated by the IMF further deepened the crisis. The effects of the Asian Crisis remain today in the depreciated currencies and social instability of some of the affected countries. The turmoil and bitterness brought on by the Asian Crisis and subsequent crises in Russia and Latin America led many people to question and even reject the idea of globalisation which they mistakenly identified with the free flow of capital only. Globalisation has also come under attack by various groups for other reasons.

Reasons to globalise

Why do companies and nations globalise? The bottom-line is profits of course—for both companies and countries, advanced and developing. The best way to make profits is to specialise in something one can do best in and to trade one's products for other products that one cannot make or at least cannot make well. For example, DMIB (formerly Dunlop Malaysia Industries Bhd.) is very good at making tyres. DMIB probably can make and sell tyres cheaper and faster than any other company in Malaysia. But DMIB may not be very good at transporting goods. So DMIB concentrates on producing tyres and lets a shipping company like NOL or Maersk transport the tyres it makes to its markets (for example, in Europe).

If DMIB were to limit itself to just the Malaysian market, then its profits would also be limited by the number of tyres that can be sold to customers in Malaysia. DMIB can increase its profits if it can also sell its tyres to other countries, say in Europe. Profitable companies provide jobs for the people. The taxes they pay help make the country rich. The support industries these profitable companies spawn generate even more jobs and taxes for the country.

Like companies, different countries have different resources and advantages. Countries can capitalise on their relative advantages to produce goods and services that other countries will buy. By specialising, companies and countries become better than others in their chosen fields. Their productivity is therefore higher too, i.e., they can produce their goods and services cheaper and faster than others can. The surplus can then be traded for other goods that they cannot produce efficiently. Malaysia is very good at producing palm oil which it can sell for goods it cannot produce, for example, a squadron of MiG-29 fighter planes from Russia. Advanced countries prefer to specialise in making more value-added and sophisticated goods and services partly because their populations want and can afford them. Selling such goods and services is far more profitable and allows advanced countries to trade them for the lower-value goods they no longer want to make from developing countries. Therefore specialisation and trade are the basic building blocks of corporate and national prosperity for everyone. Globalisation—a term that has become popular—merely refers to the vastly increased speed and ease of conducting trade due to advances in transportation, communications and information technology in the last 20 years.

Implications for the future

The vast majority of countries in the world today accept globalisation eagerly or reluctantly depending on how able and willing they are to embrace the prerequisites of free trade, industrialisation and technology flow. Although few countries dare to reject globalisation outright because the benefits it can bring are so clear and immense, not everyone has or will benefit from globalisation. The explosive growth in international trade has mainly benefited the Newly Industrialising Economies (NIEs) of Hong Kong, South Korea, Singapore and Taiwan, which trebled their share of world trade from 3 per cent in 1971 to 9 per cent in 1999. By contrast, the Middle Eastern countries did not increase their share at all, while Africa's share actually declined from about 3.5 per cent to 1.5 per cent. Malaysia had become the sixth largest exporter of manufactured goods in the world by the mid-1990s. This did not happen by accident. The fruits of globalisation go to those who understand what globalisation is all about and are willing to rise to its challenges. While Malaysia was lucky in having rich natural resources, the main reason for its success so far has been the relatively enlightened policies followed by every government since after World War II. Each government has committed unwaveringly to open trade and depended on the private sector to bring about economic growth. The main protection the government extended to local manufacturers is tariffs on foreign products and even these have usually been low and are decreasing steadily. Neither did the government compete with the private sector in manufacturing—except in a few politically sensitive but unprofitable heavy industries which the private sector would have steered clear of anyway. This government-led attempt into heavy industrialisation in the 1980s was an attempt to replicate the successes of South Korea and Japan. After the recession of 1985, the emphasis switched from heavy industrialisation to export-oriented industrialisation. Malaysia has made the transition from primary commodity production to export-oriented manufacturing of labour-intensive goods with great success. Nevertheless, past performance is no guarantee of future performance. In a globalised economy, Malaysia now has to move up into capital and technology-intensive manufacturing if it is to become a truly developed nation. There are many challenges ahead and below are just a few we should watch out for.

Globalisation is global competition

When every country is striving to sell its products and services, then buyers have many choices. As in the local market, so it is with the global market; the customers will look for the best deal in terms of price and quality of both the goods and the services. Exporters will have to be very competitive in terms of quality, price and service to get and keep a share of the market. The quality of the goods is usually standardised to internationally accepted standards because of competitive pressures in the market. Buyers from across the world have a clear expectation of what they will be getting even though the seller they choose to buy from may be half a world away. Failure or inability to meet those standards would basically put a manufacturer out of consideration, if not out of business altogether. As a result, goods traded internationally whether they are disc drives or oil are increasingly commoditised. Buyers generally get the same quality whomever they buy from. The main differentiators remaining are therefore price and quality of service.

Keeping Malaysia competitive

Price can make or break a deal. Once quality is fixed, the lower price will generally win the deal. The need to keep the price low is therefore of paramount importance for success in the global market. In a global economy, manufacturers do not have a lot of pricing power; therefore it is hard for them to manage revenue. On the other hand, it is within every company's power to manage costs. Low wages is a natural advantage of developing countries since wages are a major cost in producing many commodities. The success of Japan in the 1960s, Malaysia in the 1980s and China now in the global market is due to their low costs of labour. However, this advantage disappears over time as wages in these countries rise as their economies grow and their people become increasingly wealthy. When that happens, every country has to find other ways of meeting the challenge of how to continue manufacturing goods at internationally competitive prices and still let wages continue to rise.

Low-cost manufacturing is not the only solution. Even advanced countries keep a lot of manufacturing onshore, e.g., the U.S. still makes common and low-tech commodities like tyres. American manufacturers can still make profits in a high-wage (or high-cost) environment if productivity—the amount of goods produced per worker—is high enough. Rather than actually making the products with their hands, American workers often monitor and service machines that do the actual making, i.e., the manufacturing plants are highly automated. Often, the number of workers—and the cost of labour—required to produce the same amount of output drops significantly. Therefore to have high productivity, workers must be highly trained in order to use sophisticated tools and technology. The incentives offered by the Malaysian government with regards to on-the-job training are certainly a step in the right direction. Yet in advanced countries, a lot of training actually takes place between jobs.

Dealing with unemployment

Malaysia industrialised in the 1980s when Japan needed to move its manufacturing to locations with a lower wage structure. Today, countries like China in turn, are industrialising as the NIEs move their manufacturing to the former because of their relatively lower wage structures. This basic economic truth may be glossing over the social, political and even personal pain to come for the nations involved. The experience in advanced nations has shown that as the manufacturing base of a nation leaves for other countries on a one-way ticket, it leaves behind the workers and communities that had nurtured these industries (sometimes for generations). Some workers—especially the older ones—will find great difficulties in obtaining new employment—at least employment that allows them to maintain something resembling their old lifestyles and standards of living. Even younger workers will have problems finding new employment if they do not have the skills needed for the new jobs that become available. Entire communities can disintegrate because their sources of income, whether it was a mill or a plant, closed or moved overseas. It can take years for these countries to re-orient themselves into service-based economies.

It is not inconceivable that Malaysia and the NIEs may one day see a hollowing out of their own industrial bases. Unemployment is already rising to record levels in Japan, Hong Kong and Singapore although they are still low by Western standards. The advanced countries have learned to provide some safety nets for their unemployed workers. Unemployed workers can draw upon unemployment benefits for a fixed period of time while looking or training for a new job. Sometimes the system can be abused if money from unemployment benefits is almost the same as that derived from low-paying jobs. In the U.S. and Britain, the system was reformed to offer less financial support and the duration of the support was also reduced. Other countries like Germany and the Netherlands still have relatively generous unemployment systems but are now being forced to consider reforms because of the high costs involved. The U.S. also has government-sponsored retraining schemes for unemployed workers to help them acquire new marketable skills. Many unlucky but enterprising workers have availed themselves of this aid to change to more marketable careers and to upgrade themselves successfully. Currently, Asian countries, both NIEs and developing, have no coherent strategy for dealing with unemployment despite several recessions recently. This is because these countries' experiences with recessions have always been short. In fact, during the last 20 years, the only time Malaysia experienced deep recession was from 1985 to 1988. In such times, familial safety nets have always taken care of the unemployed during those brief recessions. However, should these countries begin experiencing a hollowing out of their manufacturing bases, then unemployment may become more persistent and the traditional familial safety nets may fail. Tiding family members over a bad spell is good on an individual level but for the country's economy as a whole, this is not the same as retraining a country's work force with new skills for new industries.

Size does matter

In the past, industries and manufacturers were protected by their own governments which imposed tariffs on cheaper imports and also limited more efficient firms from entering the local markets. This is of course detrimental to the local consumers who must pay higher prices for those products and services but this is regarded as necessary to give the local producers a chance to get themselves ready to face the competition. Yet, developing countries like Malaysia need to think carefully about the costs and duration of this nurturing. An example is the Malaysian car project. At the time of its inception 20 years ago, it was regarded as a means to accelerate the industrialisation of the country by creating demand for a host of downstream industries. Today, Proton cars command 65 per cent of the local car market and are exported in token numbers to more than 50 countries.

The small domestic market is also Proton's biggest market. Malaysia produced only 222,000 cars in 2002, which is actually a slight drop from the 254,000 produced in 2000 and 251,000 produced in 1999. That is a relatively small number compared to the 8.3 million produced by Japan. As a rule of thumb, an annual production of about 200,000 cars per production line is needed just to break even. In heavy industries, size of output does matter because high operating and research costs must be spread out over many units of production. The huge research and development (R&D) costs of designing and developing cars—RM800 million in the next two years to develop three new models alone—can only be recouped by economies of scale, i.e., spreading the cost over many units of production. A market of only 23 million people is not big enough to support such a capital-intensive industry as car manufacturing. If the Malaysian car industry is to survive, it must export in meaningful numbers. Even the Japanese carmakers, which Proton models itself after, recognise they cannot survive with just their local market of 127 million—which has been stagnating for the last 12 years. Therefore Proton's domestic achievement does not necessarily mean the Malaysian car will be competitive in the global marketplace. Malaysia had to impose import tariffs of 300 per cent on foreign cars to virtually ensure the Malaysian consumer will find the Malaysian car the best value for money. This also has the effect of artificially increasing Proton's market share and profitability all these years. While the car project has indeed created several downstream industries and there are now two indigenous car companies, the Malaysian car has not made much impact internationally. In fact, Proton's overseas operations have lost money—RM253.2 million in 2001 and RM92 million in 2002—although it may be turning around with an estimated profit of RM16 million. In contrast, the Japanese went into car manufacturing in a serious way in the 1960s and by the late 1980s, they had almost brought the American car manufacturers to their knees. Proton has yet to enter the American market and this is a matter of concern because the American car market is the largest in the world. To be fair, the American car manufacturers were complacent in the 1980s and they have since totally revamped their operations. Proton therefore has a much harder job now in trying to break into the American market. But it can be done. The Koreans began making cars in the late 1960s and began exporting in the 1980s. Despite the ravages of the Asian Crisis, the Korean carmakers are seriously challenging the Japanese carmakers for market share in America.

In 2005, the tariff protection Proton has enjoyed all these years will end with the implemention of the Asean Free Trade Area (AFTA). Foreign cars with at least 40 per cent local content will be able to compete with Proton on an equal footing. Given Malaysia's relatively small car market, not that many foreign car manufacturers will rush to meet the 40 per cent local content ruling but within five or six years, Proton may lose up to half of its current market share. Unless Proton globalises—something it has not succeeded yet in all its 20 years of existence—it will face the equivalence of slow strangulation. To avoid that end, Proton has set up a joint venture in China and may eventually set up engineering design and research facilities there. It is also increasing its production capacity to export to other Asean countries and began lowering costs by making engines locally. However, given the fact that Proton still cannot compete domestically without tariff protection, it would be interesting to see how it plans to compete on neutral foreign grounds against the giant U.S. and Japanese carmakers which are already entrenched in nations such as Thailand.

Profits matter even more

Size alone is no guarantee of survival, let alone success. Japan is an object lesson in this. Japan's car market is much bigger than Malaysia's. Less than 20 years ago, Japanese car manufacturers were almost spreading panic among their Western counterparts with their seemingly unbeatable quality and prices. While Honda and Toyota cars are still the bestselling cars in the U.S. today, fortune has changed for the other Japanese car manufacturers. American car manufacturers eventually fought back with better styling and accessories, new annual models, and new products like trucks and SUVs (Sports Utility Vehicles). The less nimble of the Japanese manufacturers failed to adjust quickly enough. Today, Mazda is a wholly-owned subsidiary of Ford; Suzuki and Isuzu are owned by General Motors, and

Mitsubishi Motors is now controlled by DaimlerChrysler which itself was the result of Daimler-Benz buying and taking over Chrysler. (Since Mitsubishi owns just under 16 per cent of Proton, DaimlerChrysler indirectly owns a small strategic stake in Proton too.) Nissan is now controlled by Renault (as is Korea's Samsung Motor Co.). Today, only Honda and Toyota remain independent. This rapid turn of events can be attributed to just one factor—insufficient profits. The global marketplace is a brutally competitive arena. The battle for market share often results in slim profits. The slightest misjudgment can turn slim profits into huge losses. Malaysia's attempt to build car, steel and cement manufacturing industries through joint ventures with the Japanese in the 1980s was founded on high tariff protection for these industries to give them time to become competitive. In other words, they were basically unprofitable from the start. By the late 1980s, it was estimated that Malaysia had invested over RM42 billion in these industries, which employed less than 5,000 people and had never turned a real profit. Fortunately, the government quickly reined in this subsidised industrialisation and it was the private sector's profitable labour-intensive manufacturing industries that drove the country's spectacular growth throughout the 1990s. Clearly, Malaysia needs to move up into the next stage of industrialisation but it must be done with profitability as the main goal. No nation industrialises for the sake of getting industrialised alone. After all, if there are not going to be any gains from industrialisation, why not keep our idyllic pastoral lifestyle and pristine environment? We should only go into industries where we have some degree of advantage and only after careful analysis and not underestimating the capability of our competitors or the ruthless nature of global competition. We cannot as individuals or as a nation squander precious resources in creating an artificially benign environment when our overseas competitors are going to show us no mercy.

Cooperation to spread the risk

Globalisation can bring both prosperity and technological advancement but companies and nations must be willing to cleverly play the game of globalisation. One of the main buzzwords in business today is "strategic alliances". The first instinct of companies and even nations is to go it alone. If one can succeed in something that no one else can, then one has an advantage in that field and that brings enormous profits, not to mention prestige as well. However, depending on the size of the project, the effort and resources required can go beyond what a single company or even nation can bear. And even if a company has the resources to complete a project by itself, it is bound to be slower working alone compared to competitors who may be working collaboratively to share the workload and ideas. In a globalised world, there are few rewards for coming in second, what more for the also rans. Speed will affect survival itself. Therefore to maximise the speed to bring a product to market and to spread the risks, companies and even nations collaborate as much as possible. In the U.S., independent movie studios have collaborated in producing big-budget films like *Gladiator* (DreamWorks SKG and Universal Studios) and *Toy Story I* and *II* (Walt Disney Company and Pixar Animation Studio). Tie-ups between American and Japanese car manufacturers who were once implacable rivals are now more often the norm than the exception. Through such cooperation, competing manufacturers can cut research and production and parts procurement costs by sharing "platforms", i.e., chassis, engine and other major components and streamlining manufacturing and distribution. These synergies contribute directly to both competitors' bottom line at the expense of other competitors who may still be trying to go it alone. In the next ten years, every industry—heavy or otherwise—will continue to see consolidation, i.e., companies merging to become bigger and more efficient competitors. In the U.S. today, there are just four giant accounting firms—dubbed the Final Four: Pricewater-houseCoopers, Deloitte & Touche, Ernst & Young and KPMG—dominating the marketplace. These are expected to be reduced to three in the near future simply because American regulators are unlikely to accept less than three competitors in any major industry. There would probably be just three or four microchip makers like Intel competing globally. This is a trend that has been growing for the last few decades and although the pace of consolidation may vary, the outcome is not in doubt. The idea of national pride and even nationalism itself has taken into account this new reality. The history of Asia has already played out a similar scenario during the last 200 years. When the full impact of Western science and technology hit Asia for the first time in the early 19th century, each nation was forced to react in the best way possible to that new challenge. Japan and Thailand basically decided if they couldn't beat the West, they might as well join them. China, on the other hand, with its high culture and old civilisation, decided to put national pride first. That fateful decision did not really stop China from taking its rightful place in the global community. But it delayed it for about 100 years!

We could go on and on about other challenges such as inflation, migration, and so on that Malaysia would have to face in the globalised economy. But in the final analysis, the biggest and perhaps the only challenge Malaysia has to face is whether its leaders can motivate and persuade their people to adapt to this brave new world. Malaysians have been a lucky lot thus far. The government has by and large been responsive to the needs of the people and sheltered them from the worse effects of global competition. We inherited a country with good infrastructure and economy from the British when they left and we have built on it consistently and impressively. But in many ways, this paternalistic benevolence may have made us soft and less willing to adapt to new realities. Many people complained about having to learn to use more English. Others complained that they are not given scholarships to study overseas for their first degree. We need to remember that foreign investors do not have to invest in Malaysia in the first place because other nations are more than happy to give them what they want. Global competition begins right inside our individual houses: are each of us individually as productive, well-trained and adaptable as our counterparts across the border or on the other side of the globe? If the answer is no, we should lose no time in redressing our deficiencies because nobody will wait to give us a second chance.

What if we don't want to globalise?

If we Malaysians are happy enough with our current lot, we don't have to globalise. Large parts of Africa are not integrated into the global economy. Their people live and work and have families just like people everywhere else. Nearer home, we only have to look at countries like Laos and Mongolia that for one reason or another cannot or do not want to be fully integrated into the global economy. Their people live and work too—happily presumably or we would have heard of unrest or conflict from these countries. Naturally, there is a price to be paid for not taking part in globalisation just as there is a price to be paid for taking part in globalisation. The people in these countries may not be so well-off in terms of material wealth or creature comforts but who are we to say that they are less happy than us for that? The choice in front of the Malaysian people today is whether the *benefits* of globalisation outweigh the *problems* of globalisation—and whether we want these benefits badly enough to pay the price of participation.

Chapter 15

New Skills for Professional Success in the Globalised 21st Century

"GLOBALISATION" refers to the increasing economic integration of the nations of the world through international trade, investment, production, currency trading and so on. The influence of new communication and transportation technologies and the role played by multinational corporations (MNCs) in the spread of globalisation are widely recognised. Some observers have also pointed out the impact of globalisation on local norms, values and behaviour.

Certain academicians argue that globalisation is not a new phenomenon since global trade, investment and labour migration were already significant at the end of the 19th century. According to this view, contemporary globalisation is not something new but only qualitatively different because of advances in technology and

organisation that result in "space-time compression".
Space-time compression means that vast geographic
distances and time zone differences are being surmounted
by high speed travel, movement of large amounts of goods
over long distances at relatively low cost and in a timely
fashion, and convenient high speed communication and
transmission of data and information. These technological
advances have facilitated transnational economic activities
and therefore speeded up the rate and extent of
contemporary globalisation.

Globalisation and the business executive or professional

What does globalisation imply for the business executive or
professional of the 21st century? As the cliché goes, it
implies both opportunities as well as threats. Opportunities
in the sense that the possibilities of production for export,
foreign investment, joint ventures and strategic alliances
with foreign companies, etc. would be enhanced. Threats
in the sense that competition from foreign products and
services would become greater. There would also be stiff
competition from foreign multinational corporations that
may have significant financial, technological, product
development and managerial capability.

Corporations that produce for the local market would
need to meet world product standards in order to compete
successfully with foreign-made products, they would need
to upgrade their technology continuously, hire high-level
personnel who are "world class" and so on. If these
corporations decide to invest in foreign countries or form
joint ventures or strategic alliances, their personnel would

need many skills. The skills would include not only international finance, marketing and negotiation skills but also political savvy, diplomatic skills, linguistic skills, the ability to avoid cross-cultural misunderstandings, etc.

Individuals who work for a foreign MNC may face more demands and pressures from the international headquarters of the MNC: as MNCs rationalise their activities worldwide, local subsidiaries will be under pressure to increase profits and cut costs, contract out, downsize and delayer and so on. Thus, as globalisation continues unabated, business life would get more interesting as well as more demanding.

New skills needed for professional success in the globalised 21st century

The range of skills needed for professional success in the 21st century will be quite broad as a result of globalisation of business. Business schools and MBA programmes typically teach traditional business skills such as finance, accounting, marketing, human resource management and so on. Innovative business schools have introduced MBA programmes that focus on international business management. Thus, these schools have "internationalised" and "globalised" their curricula. Students studying such curricula may also be required to spend a semester or two in a foreign country in order to broaden their outlook and prepare them for future work as global managers. Business executives and professionals who have not been exposed to business education programmes that focus on international business will need to learn the necessary skills on their own.

International business skills include not only those skills that are taught in traditional business education programmes but also knowledge and skills that are important for professional success in a global context but that are seldom taught in business schools. Such skills and knowledge would include knowledge of the politics of foreign countries; an understanding of the norms, values and culture of foreign customers, foreign suppliers, foreign colleagues, foreign workers being managed by oneself, foreign business partners, foreign authorities, etc. Foreign language skills would also be useful for international business success.

An understanding of the norms and values of foreigners would also enhance the process of business negotiations. For example, Americans are straightforward, impatient with hierarchy, dislike cautious and drawn-out negotiations ("beating around the bush") and like to sign clear-cut contracts. Americans are thus often puzzled by "Asian" behaviour such as vagueness, deference to higher authority, avoidance of making anyone "lose face" in public, emphasis on the building of trust and the building of long-term business relationships and so on. An understanding of the values and business etiquette of different nationalities would help to facilitate international business enormously.

Books on "culture shock" and how it can affect success with respect to business activities make for amusing and eye-opening as well as (literally) profitable reading. In my opinion, they are a very informative as well as relatively painless way for the entrepreneur or manager to increase his "I.B. Quotient" (International Business Quotient) quickly.

The business executive or professional will need to be familiar with the "no-nos" and taboos of foreign societies in order to avoid committing *faux pas* or to avoid offending foreign customers, suppliers, business partners or the sensibilities of government authorities. For example, if Western corporations wish to penetrate Third World markets, they need to be aware that it is offensive to market products made from pig byproducts to Muslims, that Hindus will not eat products made from cattle and so on.

Educational systems and outlooks need to be globalised and internationalised too. This is not impossible to achieve: small European nations that are also economic powerhouses such as Switzerland, Sweden and the Netherlands are showing the way for the rest of the world. Students need to be taught to be less ethnocentric and to be more broad-minded when it comes to the subject of the norms, values, beliefs and behaviour of foreigners. Such training can only help them as they deal with foreigners in the years ahead. Students need to be taught that, in the future, they are likely to work for foreign-owned corporations operating locally. Even if they work for homegrown corporations, they are likely to deal with foreign business partners and they may also be posted overseas as managers of MNCs operating overseas.

Personnel who have been assigned to live and work in foreign countries will need to develop adequate coping skills as well as the ability to adjust to life in a foreign (and often very different) environment. These skills are not taught in schools and universities and therefore need to be learned individually. Those who have lived or studied abroad are relatively advantaged compared to those who have not had the opportunity to do so. An extended period of time spent as a student in a foreign country enables one to deal more easily with foreigners from that particular country when one becomes a professional working adult.

Thus, in our opinion, the effective professional of the 21st century would definitely need to possess "effective functioning in foreign environment" skills. These range from personal skills (e.g., an open mind, adaptability, quick adjustment to culture shock) to interpersonal skills. By interpersonal skills, we mean the ability to manage a dissatisfied or even unhappy spouse who has followed one to a posting in a foreign land, children who are having trouble adjusting to life in an alien environment, coming to terms with incidents of xenophobia, dealing with foreign bosses and colleagues, managing foreign workers in their own country, dealing with foreign business partners and foreign authorities, etc.

Those who have studied or lived overseas can remember how they had to adjust to the culture shock they experienced as foreigners in an alien environment, e.g., they may have experienced surprise or shock at how the locals differ so much in their norms, values, beliefs and behaviour. Western women may find the way in which women are treated in certain Middle Eastern, African or East Asian countries to be very difficult to accept.

Interpersonal skills
in foreign environments

Earlier, we mentioned the challenge of managing dissatisfied or unhappy spouses and children while working in a foreign land. There are some writers who believe that an unhappy spouse is a major reason for failure in an overseas job posting. Thus, managers who are posted overseas need to be aware of this challenge if they want to perform effectively overseas.

Individuals who work overseas may also experience incidents of xenophobia. Thus, it is necessary to be able to cope with incidents of xenophobia when these unpleasant events occur to oneself or to one's spouse or children.

A useful skill that a person working overseas needs to have is tact or diplomacy. As an alien working in a foreign country, one needs to be careful not to offend one's local boss, colleagues or subordinates. Thus, one may need to be very diplomatic when talking about local politics, local religious beliefs and practices, the foreign policy of the country one is working in, etc.

Professionals working overseas also need to understand how the local political system works and how to handle the local authorities (politicians, police, etc.). In certain countries, access to local politicians and other influential people can help to facilitate business transactions considerably. In other countries, petty corruption and even high-level corruption is widespread and the professional is likely to be faced with an ethical dilemma when he is expected to make "under the counter" payments or give expensive presents in order to get business going. In such cases, the counsel of local business partners and local advisers can be of enormous help.

The challenges brought about by globalisation for business executives and professionals are great indeed. However, they are impossible to avoid and therefore, new skills such as those discussed above need to be developed or acquired in order to meet these challenges successfully.

Suggested Reading

Crouch, Harold, *Government and Society in Malaysia* (St. Leonards, New South Wales, Australia: Allen and Unwin, 1996)

Friedman, Thomas, *The Lexus and the Olive Tree: Understanding Globalization* (New York: Farrar, Straus and Giroux, 1999)

Gomez, Edmund Terence and Jomo K.S., *Malaysia's Political Economy: Politics, Patronage and Profits* (Cambridge: Cambridge University Press, 1997)

Jomo K.S., *M Way: Mahathir's Economic Legacy* (Kuala Lumpur: Forum, 2003)

Khoo Boo Teik, *Beyond Mahathir: Malaysian Politics and Its Discontents* (London and New York: Zed Books, 2003)

Khoo Boo Teik, *Paradoxes of Mahathirism: An Intellectual Biography of Mahathir Mohamad* (Kuala Lumpur: Oxford University Press, 1995)

Lee Su Kim, *Malaysian Flavours: Insights into Things Malaysian* (Subang Jaya, Malaysia: Pelanduk Publications, 1996)

Stiglitz, Joseph E., *Globalization and Its Discontents* (New York, New York: W.W. Norton, 2002)

Welsh, Bridget (ed.), *Reflections: The Mahathir Years* (Washington, D.C.: Paul H. Nitze School of Advanced International Studies, Johns Hopkins University, 2004)

Index

PHUA KAI LIT teaches at the International Medical University (IMU) in Kuala Lumpur, Malaysia. He holds a B.A. in Public Health and Population Studies from the University of Rochester and a PhD in Sociology (Medical Sociology) from Johns Hopkins University. He also holds professional qualifications from the insurance industry. In 2003, he was awarded an Asian Public Intellectual Senior Fellowship from the Nippon Foundation. Before joining academia, Phua worked as a research statistician for a state health department in the U.S. and as an assistant manager for an insurance company in Singapore.

SOO KENG SOON works in the U.S. and has extensive experience in consulting on, configuring, implementing, and operating enterprise-wide eLearning management and performance management systems for multinational corporations in the U.S. and Europe with learner bases of 10 to over 100,000 remote users. He was also involved in instructional design and development for web-based, blended, skill-based learning, and performance measurement. He taught and researched in universities in Malaysia for 13 years. His current research interest is knowledge management.